Daniel Radcliffe
No Ordinary Wizard

SIMON SPOTLIGHT

An imprint of Simon & Schuster Children's Publishing Division
1230 Avenue of the Americas New York, New York 10020
Copyright © 2005, 2008 by Simon & Schuster, Inc. All rights reserved, including the right
of reproduction in whole or in part in any form.
SIMON SPOTLIGHT and colophon are registered trademarks of Simon & Schuster, Inc.
Designed by Giuseppe Castellano
Manufactured in the United States of America
2 4 6 8 10 9 7 5 3 1
ISBN-13: 978-1-4169-6771-2
ISBN-10: 1-4169-6771-0
Library of Congress Catalog Card Number 2008930263

Daniel Radcliffe
No Ordinary Wizard

by Grace Norwich

Simon Spotlight

New York   London   Toronto   Sydney

Table

Dan's Magic

1

When the millions of Harry Potter fans out there think of the sweet, unassuming boy wizard they have grown to love, a picture of Daniel Radcliffe immediately pops into their heads. That's because Dan— as all his friends and family members call him—is the young actor who, at age eleven, won the role of Harry Potter in the first movie and has been the face of the famous wizard on-screen ever since!

So just how similar is Dan to the famous wizard we all know and love? Well, quite similar, actually. Except for his lack of magical powers, Dan has a lot in common with the fictional character that has made him a household name. First off, they are both British, and very cute! But there are a lot of other, somewhat less obvious, characteristics that they share. According to Dan, they seem to have so much in common he has even joked that one day he'll have to go into therapy because every time he reads J. K. Rowling's books he finds more links between his and Harry's personalities. Not that the two boys share any bad traits. In fact, it's just the opposite!

"We have curiosity [and] loyalty," Dan told *People* magazine—two very important attributes to have. Despite his ever-rising celebrity status, Dan has managed to remain pretty levelheaded, and becoming famous hasn't at all changed the way he treats his friends and loved ones or lessened the time he makes for them in his life. Actually, whenever he gets a chance on the movie set, Dan keeps in touch with his school chums by telephone, e-mail, or text messaging. Just as Harry sniffed out Draco Malfoy at the beginning of their first year at Hogwarts, Dan also has no trouble spotting the wrong sort of people. He knows how essential it is to keep sight of the important things in life. Instead of getting wrapped up in his fame, Dan, like Harry, keeps his head out of the clouds and devotes his time to the "right" sort of people, the friends who have always stood by him, movie star or not.

Another similarity that Dan and the fictional wizard seem to share is a level of wisdom and maturity that is beyond their years, which is probably due to the fact that they both had to handle a great deal of responsibility at such a young age. While Harry has the special lightning-bolt scar that means he will have to single-handedly battle the forces of evil and save the world, Dan has had his own earthly challenges. The Harry Potter books and movies have all been such huge hits that there is hardly a corner of the globe that hasn't been touched by the unprecedented phenomenon. Because of this, an insane media storm, usually reserved only for the top echelon of A-list celebrities such as Tom Cruise and Brad Pitt, has surrounded Dan as he has grown from a skinny, small kid to the hunky teenager he is today. Throughout his time in the spotlight, however, Dan has proved himself to be as gracious and professional as any adult.

Not that Dan, or Harry, for that matter, is always a choirboy. They both partake in their fair share of mischief—just ask any of the other actors on the Harry Potter sets who have been on the receiving end of Dan's practical jokes. But they never take it too far. Although they both "get in trouble," as Dan told *People*, "we don't break the rules, we just kind of bend them."

Moviegoers watching Harry Potter escape one hair-raising adventure after another may think they know Dan Radcliffe. Sometimes it's so easy to get swept up in the magic and mania of Harry Potter that people start thinking of Dan and the fictional character he plays on-screen as one and the same. But let the record show, despite their similarities, Dan is different from the character he plays in many ways. Just as Clark Kent took off his glasses to unveil Superman, when Dan takes off his trademark Harry Potter spectacles and that snug Hogwarts blazer, he reveals his true self. When he is not battling the forces of evil on the big screen, Dan likes to kick back and listen to music by the Sex Pistols or New York Dolls—brash, loud punk music one wouldn't associate with such a soft-spoken and polite boy. And he's got a lot of other tricks up his sleeve. Let's discover the magic that has made Dan Radcliffe into one of the hottest, most talented young stars in the world.

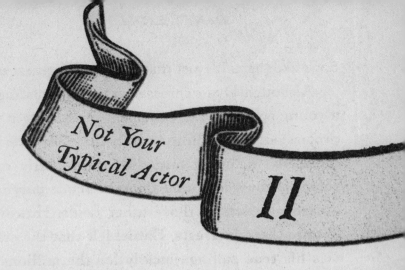

Not Your Typical Actor

II

Daniel Jacob Radcliffe was born on July 23, 1989, in London, England, to Alan Radcliffe and Marcia Gresham. He grew up in the well-to-do neighborhood of Fulham, in the southwest part of the city. Daniel attended Sussex House, an exclusive all-boys private school in Chelsea, where his favorite classes were gym and science. Dan has always been an individual, not one to follow the crowd. At an early age he didn't associate with the in-group, but rather rooted for the kind of underdog that he would later come to embody playing the character of Harry Potter. "I've never been one of the cool people at school, but then again, I don't get the people who are cool," Dan told the Associated Press in an interview. Not one to comfortably bad-mouth anyone, even school snobs, he added, "It's not that I don't like them. It's just that they don't interest me."

Although Dan expressed interest in acting at a young age, he wasn't dead set on making it his profession. As a young boy Dan had many other interests, including medicine, particularly neurological disorders, and thought about pursuing a career in one of those other fields. However, despite these interests, Daniel felt that the stage was his true calling—luckily for the millions of fans who currently adore him. His very first acting experiences were in small school productions. "My earliest memory of acting was playing a monkey in a school play, when I was about six," Dan told E! Online. "I had floppy ears and orange makeup, and I had to wear tights. I think I went on and danced around for about forty seconds or something. I hope nobody ever digs up a picture of me in that, because it was embarrassing."

School plays were a beginning, but Dan learned more about the world of professional acting from a source much closer to home: his parents. His father, Alan, was a literary agent, and his mother, Marcia, was a casting director. In the beginning of her career, Marcia turned her creative energy toward theater and produced some plays, until eventually she set up her own casting agency. Marcia forged a successful career, taking on the position of casting director on many well-known British productions, including the series *The Inspector Lynley Mysteries* for television and a recent made-for-TV drama called *The Government Inspector*. Alan had also tried his hand at acting. He trained for the theater at an acting school in Guildford. But he eventually gave it up and went to work as an agent for International Creative Management, one of the world's largest talent and literary agencies.

Because of their professions and interest in the arts, the Radcliffes socialized in industry circles, rubbing elbows with high-level professionals who worked in television, theater, and film. And these people really knew the business; they could tell you exactly what would work and what wouldn't. It almost seemed inevitable that one of these well-trained, seasoned professionals would discover Dan's potential. Sure enough, a family friend suggested to Alan and Marcia that Daniel would be good for the title part in a television production of *Oliver Twist*. Dan was excited at the prospect and really wanted to give it a shot, but Alan and Marcia were reluctant to allow Dan to enter the world of professional acting. Being involved in the performing arts themselves, they were aware of the pressures and sacrifices that go with being a professional child actor. They worried about Daniel missing out on a normal childhood; they feared that he might be taken advantage of or pressured into adopting a lifestyle of intense work and grueling hours at too young an age. They did not want the decision they made to be one that they would later regret. And so, the opportunity for *Oliver Twist* came and went, and Daniel remained undiscovered.

Who knows how Dan convinced his parents to say yes the next time an opportunity came around— maybe he begged for hours, or maybe he just flashed them those big blue eyes. But when they later found out that a friend of theirs, Kate Harwood, was set to produce another Charles Dickens tale, *David Copperfield*, for the British Broadcasting Corporation (BBC), they eased their strict stance and sent Harwood a picture of Dan. Needless to say, that photo got him called in for an audition. However, while his innocent face and those big baby-blues may have gotten him the audition, his good looks didn't get him the role. He had to go through five nerve-racking tryouts before he landed the part in 1999.

Dan was only ten years old at the time, and he had never even read any of Dickens's novels. Although he enjoyed hearing some of the stories that had been written by the quintessential Victorian author, Daniel was way more impressed by Pokémon, *The Simpsons*, and the Macaulay Culkin film *Home Alone*. "Now that's really funny," he told the *Boston Herald*, referring to the classic kid flick. What's even funnier is that only about a year later, Daniel would wind up working with the director of that movie!

Although Dan's part in *David Copperfield* was his first professional role, he was already working alongside some of the best actors in the business. The cast included Dame Maggie Smith as Aunt Betsey. Maggie, who would work with Dan again about a year later in the first Harry Potter film, had been in the business for more than forty years. The cast also included Bob Hoskins, who played Micawber. Bob Hoskins had been in the business for more than twenty-five years. Sir Ian McKellen, who played the mean schoolmaster, Creakle, was also one of England's most renowned actors.

It's hard to imagine how intimidating it must have been for Dan when he first walked onto the set. This BBC production, filled with veteran actors, was a far cry from his performance as a dancing monkey. Dan told the *Boston Herald* in 2000, "On the first day it was really scary. I was afraid I would do something wrong or mess up my lines." Even the director, Simon Curtis, realized how tough it must have been for young Dan. "It was kind of weird at times to be directing some of the greatest actors in the world with the newest actor in the world," Curtis told the *Boston Herald*. But Dan wasn't chosen because of his résumé, he was chosen because of his talent. It just happened to be a bonus that Dan ended up being "a perfectly delightful boy," as Curtis told the *Boston Herald*.

David Copperfield premiered on the BBC in England on Christmas Day of 1999. Although it might seem odd that they chose Christmas Day as the date for the film's television premiere, it was actually a very wise and calculated decision. In Britain, Christmas Day television-watching is as much of a tradition as is eating mince pies, and on this widely celebrated holiday, viewer ratings sky-rocket. Airing *David Copperfield* on Christmas was not only an honor, but a guarantee that it would be seen in millions of homes across Britain. The film aired in America on *Masterpiece Theatre* on PBS later the following year.

Although he was the youngest and least experienced cast member, Dan's performance in the television film gained him glowing reviews from critics, who easily recognized natural talent. In the *Christian Science Monitor*, one reviewer wrote, "The real heartthrob in this piece, though, is young Radcliffe as the child Davey—who is real as rain. Those wonderful eyes and cherubic face make us feel every thorn and every joy with equal truth." That is the kind of review that some actors wait years and years to receive, and Daniel earned it after his very first performance!

After *Copperfield*, Dan didn't rush into a full-time acting career. He returned to his regular life of going to school, playing Pokémon, and listening to music. But his innate talent for acting couldn't grow within the confines and limitations of his school plays anymore. Soon enough Dan landed another professional role, and this time the part was in a major feature film called *The Tailor of Panama*.

Once again, Daniel found himself working alongside two legendary actors, Geoffrey Rush and

Jamie Lee Curtis, who played his parents in the film. Ironically, while on set, Jamie Lee told Dan's mom that she thought he looked a lot like the fictional character Harry Potter. . . .

Dan had demonstrated pretty quickly that he could be a success in show business, but still his parents were hesitant about his becoming a professional actor. Alan and Marcia wanted to shield their son from the struggling and suffering that the typical actor must overcome. The one thing that Alan and Marcia forgot to consider was the fact that Daniel had no intention of being typical.

Harry Potter Mania

III

While Dan was honing his skills as a young actor, Harry Potter was rapidly becoming a worldwide phenomenon. J. K. (short for Joanne Kathleen) Rowling first imagined the character of Harry in 1990, while she was stuck on a train for four hours somewhere between Manchester and London. "Harry just strolled into my head fully formed," J. K. told Scholastic.com in an interview.

Born near Bristol, England (a few miles from a town called Dursley, which should sound familiar since it's the name of Harry Potter's muggle relatives), J. K. always had her head in far-off places and imaginary lands. She started writing stories when she was only six years old, but her road to becoming a professional writer was as topsy-turvy as one of Harry Potter's adventures.

On that fateful train where she thought up the character that would eventually inspire her world-famous series, J. K. couldn't even find a piece of paper or a pen. So she kept all the details of her newfound idea in her head until she returned home and could write them down. Luckily, she didn't forget a single thing! Inspiration came at the funniest moments for J. K. While she was flying on an airplane (travel seems to spark this woman's imagination), the names of the Hogwarts houses—Gryffindor, Ravenclaw, Slytherin, and Hufflepuff—just popped right into her head. Again she didn't have paper, so she wrote the names on the back of a barf bag!

Developing the Harry Potter series was not an easy undertaking. She wasn't a full-time writer with a fancy desk and a quiet office to help her along. J. K. was a single mom who had to make ends meet and write in the intermittent moments while her daughter, Jessica, napped. But J. K. didn't waste much time. Even while she sat in a favorite café in Edinburgh, Nicolson's, she jotted down a lot of the book on little scraps of paper. It took her six years, but finally, the first Harry Potter book was completed.

In 1997, *Harry Potter and the Philosopher's Stone* was published, and to the delight of millions of children and their parents, a universe of witches, wizards, muggles, Quidditch, Gringotts, and fantastical creatures was born. J. K.'s American editor felt that the word "philosopher" gave an incorrect impression. He felt that the title should be more suggestive of magic, and so it became known in America as *Harry Potter and the Sorcerer's Stone*. The success of J. K.'s first book was instantaneous and amazing. It spent thirty-one weeks at No. 1 on *USA Today*'s bestselling books list. With six more books already planned out inside her head, J. K. continued to bring the story of Harry Potter and his magical world to life, and readers of all ages lined up at the door, waiting with bated breath for the moment when the new Harry Potter book would hit the shelves.

The second in the series, *Harry Potter and the Chamber of Secrets,* was published in the summer of 1998, and in the fall of that year, J. K. quickly followed with a third book, *Harry Potter and the Prisoner of Azkaban*. Sales skyrocketed with each new book, all of which made it onto the *New York Times*, *USA Today*, and *Wall Street Journal* bestseller lists. In secret warehouses the books were guarded by tight security before they went on sale. The Potter tomes flew off the shelves faster than the publisher could restock them.

On July 8, 2000, the fourth book, *Harry Potter and the Goblet of Fire*, became an unheard-of publishing sensation, selling three million books in the first forty-eight hours! *Publishers Weekly* called it "the fastest-selling book in history." The fifth in the series, *Harry Potter and the Order of the Phoenix*, had an unprecedented first print run of 6.8 million copies and a second print run of an additional 1.7 million copies. The first five books in the series spent a combined fifty-seven weeks at No. 1 on the *USA Today* list. Her sixth book, *Harry Potter and the Half-Blood Prince*—which hit bookstores July 16, 2005—broke the record set by *Order of the Phoenix* with an initial print run of 10.8 million copies, according to its U.S. publisher, Scholastic.

But all that is just child's play compared to the last book in the Harry Potter series. The release of *Harry Potter and the Deathly Hallows* on July 21, 2007, was more than just a publishing event. It blew every other of her past book releases away. Scholastic created yet another industry record when it printed 12 million copies of *Deathly Hallows* for its first U.S. print run. And that wasn't just wishful thinking on the part of publishing executives. They had done their research and knew *Deathly Hallows* would fly off the shelves. The number of Amazon.com preorders for *Deathly Hallows*, up 547 percent from the preorders for *Half-Blood Prince*, was a good indicator. They weren't disappointed by the results. *Deathly Hallows* was the fastest-selling book ever! Released in more than ninety-three countries around the world, it sold more than 11.3 million copies during its first twenty-four hours in the United States, Britain, and Germany alone! It's no surprise that the United States made up the bulk of those sales—8.3 million, to be precise. American kids just couldn't wait to see what was in store for Harry during his final chapters. And the craze didn't stay in the stores. Libraries couldn't keep the books on their shelves. One public library in Cincinnati was deluged with 2,500 requests for its 810 copies of *Deathly Hallows* before they had even arrived at the branch.

All you need to do is type in "Harry Potter" on the Internet to see how Harry Potter mania has swept the world. Part of the success of the Harry

Potter series is due to the fact that the books aren't *just* for kids. The story is so exciting and compelling, and the characters so real, that grown-ups find themselves equally absorbed in the Harry Potter tale. It's estimated that 40 percent of Rowling's readers are adults!

With the worldwide Harry Potter mania and J. K.'s overwhelming and ever-increasing fan base, there are more than 100 million copies of Harry Potter books in print in the United States, and 260 million copies distributed to more than two hundred countries in sixty-one languages worldwide, including Zulu. It was only a matter of time before Harry Potter would leap off the page and onto the big screen. And that's where it all began for Daniel.

In 1997, David Heyman, a successful English producer, picked up a copy of *Harry Potter and the Philosopher's Stone* and read the book about the famous little boy with the scar on his forehead. After reading J. K. Rowling's first bestseller, he decided that it would be the launch project for his new company, Heyday Films. But he knew from the start that in order for the books to work on-screen, any film version would have to remain faithful to J. K. Rowling's original vision.

Before any deals could be made, David had to get J. K.'s permission to move forward with the project. Luckily, J. K. was excited about the prospect of seeing her vision come to life on-screen, and optioned the rights for *Harry Potter and the Philosopher's Stone* to him and Warner Bros. for $700,000. That may seem like a ton of money, and of course it is for a regular person, but in the movie business, $700,000 is cheap, especially for the gold mine that the Harry Potter film series would become. At the time that he bought the rights to the book, David had "absolutely no idea that the first film would even work," as he later told the *Chicago Sun-Times*. He went on to say that initially he "thought it would be some medium-budget British thing that might catch on."

Boy was he in for a big surprise.

To turn J. K.'s magical vision into a movie, David's first step was to bring on Hollywood screenwriter Steve Kloves, who had written the screenplay for *Wonder Boys*. Despite his obvious talent and abilities, some people, including Steve, were concerned with how J. K. would feel. As Steve later told the *Philadelphia Inquirer*, "I didn't want her to think I was going to be in the business of destroying her baby." Well, it just so happens that one of J. K. Rowling's favorite movies is *The Fabulous Baker Boys*, which was written and directed by Steve himself!

Next David signed on Chris Columbus as the director, and they were ready to begin the massive effort of creating the magical universe that is the world of Harry Potter. Making good use of the film's $125 million budget, the amazing team of crew members began creating Hogwarts, Diagon Alley, Hagrid's hut, and everything in between. But just two short months before they were set to begin shooting the film, a vital element was still missing. They still hadn't found their Harry Potter.

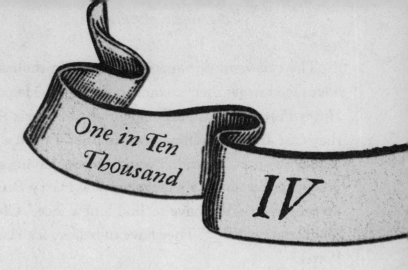

One in Ten Thousand

IV

In the fall of 1999, the producer, David Heyman, and the director, Chris Columbus, began the daunting process of casting the lead part of Harry Potter. They were positive that they would have no trouble finding someone well before the first day of filming, which was scheduled to be September 29, 2000. They were searching for someone who perfectly fit J. K. Rowling's vision. "Harry had a thin face, knobby knees, black hair and bright green eyes," she wrote about the much-beloved character in the first novel. "He wore round glasses held together with a lot of Sellotape because of all the times Dudley had punched him on the nose. The only thing Harry liked about his own appearance was a very thin scar on his forehead, which was shaped like a bolt of lightning."

The call went out and more than ten thousand boys raced to get their chance to become the famous Harry Potter. It was really important to Chris that they cast an unknown person, and not a child star, to play the part. He didn't want viewers having any preconceived notions when they saw Harry Potter up on-screen. "We have to find a new face," Chris told *Dateline NBC*. "They have to believe it's Harry Potter."

Studio executives, however, had their own ideas. They felt that getting a familiar face to play the lead character would guarantee them a hit at the box office. Chris fought the studio honchos, insisting that Harry had to be a regular kid, and on top of that, insisting that he *had* to be British. The execs were interested to see who Chris would come up with, and allowed him to continue his search for an unknown. But by July 2000, with only three months left before filming was set to begin, not one single boy, out of all the thousands who had auditioned, was thought to be right for the part.

At this point, everyone was getting panicky. "The fear was that the film would be called *Ron Weasley and the Philosopher's Stone* because there was just no Harry," David told the *Toronto Sun* in

2001. "We were down to four or five people who we thought had some of the qualities, but not all of them." A charismatic, loveable kid was crucial to the film's success, but the schedule of this very expensive production could not be held up because of this search for the Dream Harry, who might not even exist!

They were searching for "an old soul in a child's body," David explained to the *Toronto Sun*. That task seemed so impossible that one casting director simply quit out of frustration. Other casting directors were thinking of following suit, and one turned to Chris one day exasperated, and said, "I don't know what you want." He replied by handing her a tape of none other than Dan in *David Copperfield*. "This is what I want," he told her.

Unfortunately, it wouldn't be as simple as Chris had hoped. The casting director already knew for a fact that Dan's parents weren't going to let him try out for the part. Dan's parents still had the same opinion of professional acting—and their son's involvement in it—as they'd had when he had auditioned for *David Copperfield* and *The Tailor of Panama*. "I kind of had a tendency to get my hopes up," Dan said on the *Today* show in 2001. "They knew that there were thousands of boys going up for the part, so they didn't want me to get my hopes up and then be disappointed, so they were just protecting me."

Then fate took over. One summer evening Dan went to the theater with his parents to see *Stones in His Pockets*, a comedy about two extras on a big American movie shooting in Ireland. In the row directly in front of the Radcliffe family were two men who knew his father. And they were behaving oddly. Instead of concentrating on the play in front of them, the men kept turning around to stare at Dan. Did he have a stain on his tie or broccoli in his teeth? What could be more interesting than the show they had bought tickets for? "I didn't know who they were," Dan told the *Christian Science Monitor* in 2001. "But my dad asked if I'd like to go to the studio and have lunch with them."

The two men turned out to be none other than David Heyman and the screenwriter, Steve Kloves. At that lunch, Dan got a glimpse of the world that millions of kids would have done anything to see. He toured the sets and got a chance to watch the crew, who were constructing the Hogwarts School of Witchcraft and Wizardry. Needless to say, he had a lot of fun. Dan also had a brief interview with the film's producers and director, and impressed everyone enough to be asked to come back and audition for the role of Harry Potter.

For his audition Dan was asked to do three screen tests, one of which was on a broomstick! One of the scenes he read was the part when Harry, Hermione, and Ron discover that Hagrid is hiding a contraband dragon's egg. "He got me to improvise about that scene," Dan told Masterpiece Theatre Online. "He kept fumbling the lines . . . to see what I would do." Most adult actors, let alone child actors, would have crumbled in that kind of situation. "I was totally scared out of my wits. It was so terrifying," Dan told E! Online. "You go in there with these really important people, and you really feel small." However, if Dan was nervous at all, he never showed it. The day after his third screen test, he got the most important phone call of his young life. Dan was in the bathtub, of all places, when his dad came in and told him the good news: He had landed the part! What was Dan's reaction to the news? As he told the *Christian Science Monitor,* "I was Harry Potter. I was so happy, I cried."

The first thing Dan did was call both his

grandmothers, who were very excited for him. Dan was excited too, as well he should have been, and could hardly sleep at all that first night. In fact, he woke up at 2:00 a.m. and ran into his parents' room to ask them if it was all just a big, happy dream. No, they said, it's real. And then told him to go back to bed. It was pretty late, after all.

Apparently the executives who had originally wanted a big name were just as convinced of Daniel's potential as Chris was, and on August 21, 2000, Warner Bros. formally announced that the eleven-year-old English actor Daniel Radcliffe was set to play Harry Potter. The news spread like wildfire on the Internet, on television, and in the newspapers. Everyone was buzzing with talk of the new face of Harry Potter. While Dan's parents were worried about their son being thrust into the limelight, Dan was worried about how his friends would take the news. Fortunately, they were all very cool about it. "I didn't actually tell any of my friends. I was going to, but they phoned me first because they had seen it on the news . . . they reacted so well and none of them—not one single person—was jealous," he told PBS Online.

Perhaps the reason everyone was so happy for

Dan was because he kept his humble, low-key attitude, despite the fact that the news about him was
circulating fast. So humble, Dan couldn't even
understand why he had gotten the role in the first
place. "I don't know why they chose me," Dan said
on the *Today* show in 2001. "But I'm glad they did."

Chris couldn't have been happier. From the
moment he saw *David Copperfield*, Chris knew
Dan would be perfect for the role, and Dan had
turned out to be everything he had hoped. "There's
such a sense that he has lived a life, a much more
mature life than most kids his age," Chris told the
Detroit News of Daniel. "There's just such depth
in his eyes." That kind of look is usually reserved
for kids who have seen a lot of trouble in their
lives, which couldn't have been further from Dan's
experiences in his nurturing family environment.
Chris was shocked by the complexity the young
actor displayed, "because he comes from two very
loving parents who support him and who keep him
real and keep him grounded," he commented to
CNN. However, that is the test of an actor's talent
and abilities, and it was clear that Daniel passed
this test with flying colors. It became apparent
very early on that Daniel would amaze them in

many more ways in the years to come.

But what would J. K. Rowling, the ultimate Harry Potter expert, think of Dan? When she received the tape of Dan's audition performance, she called David Heyman. This phone call was a crucial moment. What would happen if J. K. Rowling did not think Daniel was right for the part? Would they have to recast Harry? It all rested on this one phone call. David shared their conversation with the *Detroit News*, describing her voice as wavering with emotion when she told him, "I feel like I've reunited with my long-lost son." Dan could not have received a bigger endorsement.

With J. K.'s approval and the role officially, one hundred percent his, Dan had to spend some serious time with the first three big books. He admitted to the *Detroit News* in 2001, "I never really enjoyed reading." Like most kids in Britain, Dan had read the first two Harry Potter books when he was about eight and nine years old. He liked them fine, but truthfully, he has admitted to the *Detroit News*, "I wasn't obsessed." But after he got the part, it was a different story. He dove back into J. K. Rowling's books and read the first three all over again. "*Now* I'm obsessed," he said. He loved them so much the second time around that he credits them with helping him read more in general. "They've really helped me to branch off into other books," he said on *Today*.

The books also helped him with his acting. Dan told Katie Couric on *Today* that figuring out how to play Harry Potter was a breeze, since J. K. had put everything down in writing. "You don't necessarily have to put . . . your own twist to it, because it's such a well-defined character in the books," he confessed. "All the explanation you need to play—it's really in the book. So I don't have to do much work, really."

That's what Dan said, but he had no idea what was in store for him once he met up with the entire crew and cast, including eleven-year-old Rupert Grint, who was cast to play Ron Weasley, and ten-year-old Emma Watson as Hermione Granger. J. K. gave her blessing to them all, telling the *San Francisco Chronicle*, "I wish Dan, Emma, and Rupert the very best of luck and hope that they have as much fun acting the first year at Hogwarts as I had writing it."

V
Film Wizards

There was no question that Dan was a mature kid, an old soul in a child's body, as David Heyman had wished for. But millions of discerning and skeptical Potter fans of all ages were waiting to be convinced that Dan could live up to the fictional character they all adored. For many kids, Harry Potter was a hero, a symbol of goodness and a fighter of evil. Fans feared that the Harry they would see on-screen would fall short of their expectations and shatter the character they loved, but at the same time they hoped Dan would prove their fears wrong and give them the real-life Harry they all wanted to see. That's a lot of pressure for an eleven-year-old kid to handle!

Dan had been so swept up in the excitement of getting the role and rehearsing with his new cast mates and director that he almost forgot about the outside pressures and social expectations associated with the huge project. But it all kind of hit him right at the moment when he needed to be at the top of his game—the first day of shooting. He got really nervous while the makeup artist was applying the famous Harry Potter scar to his head. Up until that point, he had just been doing read-throughs of the script with Rupert, Emma, and Chris in Chris's office. No big deal. But now he glanced down at the call sheet for the first day of filming and read his name, Rupert's, and Emma's. Then he turned the page and read EXTRAS, 150.

"At that moment, I got quite scared," he admitted to BBC Online. As he explained to E! Online, "I realized I was about to step in front of the camera with hundreds of people around." Dan had hit the big time: Lights! Camera! Action!

The fact that Dan had J. K. Rowling's stamp of approval almost made the pressure worse. As he told CNN later, in 2001, he hoped that he didn't go in there and "just kind of muck it up completely." He had a right to be nervous. There were the millions of expectant fans and the rumors running rampant on Harry Potter websites and in chat rooms, all about who this Daniel person was and whether or not he could hack it as the famous Harry. And there he was, young Dan, his stomach churning as he sat calmly and quietly at the center of a $125 million production. On a production that big, "mucking it up" wasn't really an option.

An army of cast and crew members was enlisted on the set of *Harry Potter and the Philosopher's/ Sorcerer's Stone*, which starts with Harry living under the stairs in his aunt and uncle's house. That's until the giant Hagrid comes to invite him to Hogwarts School of Witchcraft and Wizardry, where he not only meets his best friends but also learns about his magical powers and the truth about his parents. There were sixteen hundred crew members putting together the sets and assisting in the filming. That's not even counting all the people working in the special-effects houses, who created all the monsters and magic that looked so real in the film.

The film was shot in England, where labor laws limit the number of hours child actors can work per day. Usually on a movie, filming will go on for twelve, sometimes fourteen hours a day. It is a truly exhausting project. But Dan, Emma, and Rupert couldn't work those hours. That meant that the filming went on much longer on this set than it does on most others, and that these folks ended up spending a whole lot of time together. In total, the first Harry Potter movie took a whopping one hundred and thirty days to shoot (some independent films are shot in two weeks!).

Leavesden Studios in Hertfordshire, England, once a World War II aircraft-assembly plant, was transformed into the mammoth sets that made up the film's magical atmosphere. According to production designer Stuart Craig (who won three Oscars, including one for his work on *Gandhi*), it took the equivalent of thirty-one years in manpower to make the Hogwarts School set. The plaster was pouring. In fact, more of that stuff was used in *Philosopher's/Sorcerer's Stone* than was used to create the sets in the Roman-era epic *Gladiator*.

From scratch, crew members built the elaborate Great Hall that was big enough to fit three hundred and fifty little wizards-in-training. When all was said and done and the Great Hall came to life, J. K. was immensely pleased with what she saw. Although she was consulted often on the film, she only visited the set once. "There are, for sure, going to be people out there who are going to say that 'this is not my Great Hall,'" she told the *Philadelphia Inquirer* in 2001.

"But I can promise them, it is *my* Great Hall."

The craftsmanship of the Diagon Alley set was so detailed and complex that it easily could have been mistaken for a real street. No detail was spared. In Wiseacres Wizarding Equipment shop, a sign told customers that dragon liver and clabbert pustules were the special of the day. The Ollivanders wand shop, another boutique in Diagon Alley, was stocked with more than sixteen thousand wand boxes and had its very own fancy shopping bags that the set dresser had created. Harry Potter fans are detail junkies and wouldn't have settled for less. In fact, because the book has two different titles, two versions were shot of every single scene where the stone is mentioned.

The prop that gave the real-life wizards behind the film's production a major headache was the Whomping Willow (which inspired its own website). The violent tree is planted in the middle of the school grounds and, as is revealed later on in the series, hides an opening to a secret passage that goes from Hogwarts to the Shrieking Shack in the wizarding village of Hogsmeade. The tree, which the Weasleys' flying car eventually smashes into, was a complex combo of hydraulics and special effects.

One of the most involved scenes in the film is the amazing Quidditch game where Harry and the rest of his schoolmates ride around on broomsticks, trying to keep from getting their heads knocked off by balls known as Bludgers, while Harry tries to accomplish the goal of catching the winged Golden Snitch. That game, which practically zips by in the movie, lasting about nine minutes in total, took three months to plan and another six whole months to shoot! But Dan loved every high-flying minute. "We went very fast, very high, and I really was sitting on a broom," he told the *Detroit News* in 2001. Other than the fun he had, Dan's lips were sealed about the scene's secret special effects. But he did reveal that his favorite prop from the film was the Nimbus Two Thousand, his speedy flying broomstick. Why that one? "It is the fastest broom you can buy and makes all of Harry's friends and people who aren't so friendly to him very, very jealous," he revealed on *Today.*

The amazingly rendered sets and special effects were combined with real footage from some beautiful—and very old—places around England, including the Bodleian Library, Christ Church College, and Gloucester Cathedral. Filming at real places gave the film an authenticity that couldn't be matched by even the most skilled of production designers.

They also shot at Alnwick Castle in Scotland and in Dan's hometown of London. There, at King's Cross Station, they filmed the scene where Harry walks through a brick pillar to Platform 9¾ so he can catch the Hogwarts Express that leaves from the station only once a year. Even though Dan was filming right in the city where he lived, he still could only keep in touch with friends via e-mail and text messages. Between shooting, getting tutored on set, and returning home to sleep, there was no time for Dan to fool around with friends from school, even if they weren't very far away.

New Friends On Set

VI

With a fantastic set and special effects in place, the only thing left to do was to fill *Harry Potter and the Philosopher's/Sorcerer's Stone* with an equally fantastic cast. The film was not only going to be shot in England, it also had to have an all-British cast. Director Chris Columbus insisted on this from the get-go. As he had said from the start, he didn't want to Americanize the distinctly British vibe of the books.

Usually the most experienced people, having proved they can carry a film, get the lead roles. But in *Philosopher's/Sorcerer's Stone*, everything was turned on its head. Absolute first-timers were paired with screen legends, and the newbies were the ones who took center stage. Out of the three young lead actors, Dan had the most film experience. And he had only made one major film at that point! Rupert and Emma were completely fresh faced. Neither had done any professional acting at all. The extent of their acting experience was in school plays. Despite their lack of experience, both Emma and Rupert seemed to blow the casting directors away with their ability to portray the characters of Hermione and Ron. What sealed the deal was the fact that they worked well with Dan on-screen. "They just fit," Chris told the *Philadelphia Inquirer*.

The three Gryffindors fit on-screen because in real life, Dan told E! Online, "We all really like each other." That's important since they had to spend so much time together during that first movie, and then eventually over the years making its many sequels. One of the threesome's favorite scenes was filmed on the Hogwarts Express: It was just the three of them surrounded by tons of candy. They got to laugh, joke, and stuff themselves with sweets without any adults, as Dan would say, to muck it up. Dan credited his good chemistry with Rupert and Emma to the similarities they each shared with their fictional counterparts. "To a certain extent, we're kind of quite like our characters," he told CBS in 2002. "Our characters bond because of who they are, and I think because we're kind of like them, we all bond the same way." Dan and Rupert became really good friends, as did their characters in the film. Sometimes it was hard to tell whether they were acting or being themselves! On occasion they even called each other Ron and Harry offscreen, instead of their real names.

It's true that the young actors' personalities reflected their on-screen characters. Dan was known to be intense and a little serious, much like Harry, with the weight of the world on his shoulders. However, like Harry, Dan isn't afraid to take risks, and he knows when a good practical joke is in order.

Unlike Dan, who didn't take to the Potter books right away, Emma had already read them through and knew the material backward and forward, much like her character Hermione would have. In fact, Emma was already a crazy fan when casting agents showed up at her school to offer her and a couple of her classmates the chance to audition in the school gym. She was ecstatic when she landed the part of Hermione, a real know-it-all and the smartest student at Hogwarts. On set it took Emma longer to warm up to people, just like her reluctant character Hermione. The Oxford, England, native could, at times, have seemed cold, but that was just until she got to know everyone. It couldn't have been easy being practically the only girl surrounded by hundreds of boy wizards. "I stay on my toes," Emma told *Teen People* magazine in 2002. "Dan and Rupert make funny faces when I'm shooting. But I keep them in line." She was grateful for her friends and family, who kept her grounded to her familiar past. Maybe that's why she spent a lot of time keeping in touch with her buds by phone or e-mail. "They have treated me as a normal person," she said of her friends. "They know me as Emma. They don't go around calling me Hermione Granger. My parents have been really good about this."

Rupert was a natural ham with great comic instincts. The good-natured redhead dove right into every aspect of the film with great relish, even the part where he gets soaked by Fluffy's (the huge three-headed dog) drool. "It was kind of disgusting but it was wicked," he told the *Ottawa Citizen.* "But I certainly didn't taste it." He also got treated like an ordinary kid, and not a star, when he returned home to his brother and three sisters. "The little ones don't really understand," he laughed. "They just treat me as Rupert, which is good."

Although the three young actors shared a lot

in common, they each definitely had different ideas about the best part of their job, which they shared with the *Calgary Sun* in 2002. "Take away all the glamour and attention and premieres," Emma said. "It's the acting, and working with fantastic actors and directors." Rupert, ever the comedian, came up with his own answer: "The best was coughing up slugs. . . ." But Dan also had his own opinion as to the best perk of playing Harry Potter. "The best thing is playing a character who has inspired children and adults all over the world," Dan said. That's the typically mature, thoughtful answer one would expect from Dan. It seems as though the three really are very much like their Gryffindor characters!

Alongside these kids, who were coming up with their own ideas about acting for the first time, were famous actors who had been in the business for decades and decades. One of the most unlikely faces in *Philosopher's/Sorcerer's Stone* was Richard Harris, a famous Irish actor who had appeared in more than seventy films and television shows. A member of the Royal Shakespeare Company for thirty years, he had been offered the part of Albus Dumbledore, the head of Hogwarts School of Witchcraft and Wizardry, but originally turned it down. At seventy-one, the elderly actor shrank from the thought of committing to a seven-movie series. "I hate commitment," he told the *Washington Post* in 2001. He agreed only after his twelve-year-old granddaughter, Ella Harris, strong-armed him into it. "She's fanatic about Harry Potter," he remembered. "And when she heard I wasn't going to do it, she called me up and said, 'Papa, if you don't do it I'll never speak to you again.'" That worked, but she still couldn't get him to actually read the books. "Not my kind of reading," he complained. "So I got her to sit down and explain it all to me." All Harry Potter fans are thankful to Ella for convincing Richard to take on the role of the wise and lovable Albus.

Dame Maggie Smith, Dan's old pal from *David Copperfield*, also joined the cast as Professor Minerva McGonagall, head of Gryffindor House and the deputy headmistress at Hogwarts. It must have been nice for Dan to be reunited with a familiar face. Dan was quite fond of Maggie, even called her "cool" on national television! Unfortunately for Harry, Maggie's fictional character wasn't quite as "cool" as the real-life Maggie.

Alan Rickman, whose first major film was *Die Hard* in 1988, took the part of Professor Snape. Robbie Coltrane was cast as Rubeus Hagrid,

Harry's personal guardian giant and the game-keeper at Hogwarts. The 6'1" Scottish actor often plays giants—with a little help from a computer-generated image, he morphed into the enormous Mr. Hyde in *Van Helsing*. Even with the help of effects, Robbie still had to wear padding and lifts as Hagrid, and filming from low angles helped add to his bulk and giant-size height.

One might think that the acting legends and little kids wouldn't mix, but on the Harry Potter set anything could—and did—happen. The elders even tolerated Dan's pranks. One could say the set was kind of like the Gryffindor common room, except Dan was the one playing practical jokes, not the Weasley twins! One of Dan's favorite pastimes on the set was to fiddle with people's cell phones so that they were translated into foreign tongues. "Everyone on set has a mobile phone, and I found by pushing a few buttons, they could be programmed into different languages," Dan told the *Christian Science Monitor* in 2001. "I fixed Robbie's to speak in Turkish." Robbie's response was to take off after the fleet-footed boy. He didn't even come close to catching him since Robbie was still wearing his costume: a sixty-five-pound leather jacket and twenty-pound platform shoes. At least

Dan hadn't put *another* frog in Robbie's boot!

Occasionally Dan was the butt of some on-set jokes. One day Emma and Rupert got the bright idea to print out loads of little signs with clever sayings such as PULL MY HAIR, KICK ME, and I'M SICK. They cut out about ten of the little signs and stuck them all over Dan's back without his realizing what was going on. "He walked around for, I don't know, ten minutes without noticing," Emma remembered on *Today*. Everyone was laughing, and Dan, who didn't have a clue what was going on, couldn't understand why everyone was kicking him. For a stunt like that, Emma and Rupert would have lost loads of points for Gryffindor!

Between the pranks they did for fun and the hard work they put in actually filming the major motion picture, the kids also had to fit in their schoolwork. Just because you are about to become a worldwide star doesn't mean you can slack off and not do your homework. The year he made *Harry Potter and the Philosopher's/Sorcerer's Stone*, Dan missed everything but the first two weeks of regular school. So the three young actors were tutored between three and five hours a day on set. "I have the most fantastic tutor," Dan told PBS Online. "One-on-one tutoring really, really works because I got the best exams ever in my life." It's probably pretty hard to cheat, too.

Dan didn't regret missing school because he still got to see his friends (the most important part, right?) on the weekends. He also debriefed his best friend from school, Alex Berman, a Harry Potter "fanatic," on a daily basis. "I believe he's read the fourth book six or eight times, which is pretty impressive," Dan told the *Christian Science Monitor*. "Almost every night after the movie started, we'd talk on the phone, and I'd tell him what scenes we had filmed." He and Alex had a lot to talk about every night since Dan found the process of becoming Harry Potter extremely challenging and rewarding. "What I love about playing Harry is that he's a really real character . . . complicated, but he's very accessible," he later told *The Early Show*. "In some films you get . . . broadly drawn characters that are kind of one-dimensional." That wasn't true with this film, where he felt all the characters had "so many different sides."

Dan had always kept in mind the qualities that he and Harry shared and used those similarities to play Harry well. However, there were some aspects of Harry's character that Dan had to try very hard to relate to. The hardest part of becoming Harry,

Dan told CNN, was playing "somebody with no parents, who has never even known his parents, because I have a really close relationship with my parents, and we're really good friends." He needed to use his imagination to relate to the experiences of an orphan. Robbie Coltrane realized how difficult this must be for a kid, calling the task "a terrible responsibility for a [child]," as he explained to BBC Online. Robbie saw firsthand how Dan struggled to get the scenes right, when so much was riding on his performance. "It took him a wee bit longer to get the character," he told the *Philadelphia Inquirer*. "He's a nice kid—a lot like Harry, actually. And he and Rupert formed a brilliant bond, which is perfect, really, because Harry is a bit too intense at times, and Ron takes it out of him."

There was also the difficulty of acting with all the special effects. Dan had to deliver lines to people who weren't even there. "It requires a lot of concentration," Dan told Masterpiece Theatre Online. Sometimes he would get a little help. In the scenes with ghosts, Dan explains, "There was Chris Columbus and another man who are doing the voices for the ghosts and they're doing them so well that you kind of feel that they are there."

One thing he didn't have a problem with was learning his lines. "It's more the movement and the choreography and the facial expressions you use with the line," he described as the challenge to Masterpiece Theatre Online. "The lines, you keep going over them. . . . After a while they really sink in."

No matter what kind of problems arose during filming, the three young actors figured out how to overcome them, whether the solution involved humor, more hard work and practice, or the maturity to know when to turn to someone to ask for help. Richard Harris, for one, was truly impressed. He praised Dan, telling BBC Online, "Dan was so instinctive, and so right."

With praise, however, sometimes comes arrogance, and with stardom sometimes comes the highfalutin Hollywood attitude. Fortunately, it seems like these kids would much rather remain the sweet, reserved, well-mannered people they were when they first walked on the set. As Chris Columbus told the *Chicago Sun-Times*, "[Dan] has much more confidence as an actor although as a person, he's still a shy kid. He still thanks me after each take. You never get Julia Roberts thanking you after each take."

The premiere of *Harry Potter and the Philosopher's/ Sorcerer's Stone*, on November 3, 2001, marked the date that Dan's life would change forever. A huge tidal wave of attention was headed directly for this quiet and graceful young man. He really had no idea what was in store for him, and though he tried to keep his composure in the face of an uncertain future, he must have had his doubts. Would he be able to keep his cool? Or would he lose it on the red carpet? Nobody knew for sure.

The worldwide excitement was also brewing. Everyone else wanted to see the movie as well. Dan understood the magic of Harry Potter, why the film had the ability to elicit this kind of frenzied anticipation. "Not only myself, but I think everybody can relate to Harry in some way," he told the *Today* show.

"It's the idea of magic, when magic kind of comes to life, there's so much opportunity for absolutely anything to happen."

As if the built-in audience of millions of book lovers wasn't enough, the movie studio, Warner Bros., launched one of the biggest publicity campaigns in history. Billboards of Dan were plastered everywhere from London's double-decker buses to the office buildings of downtown Manhattan. Despite the publicity Dan always kept his cool, no matter how famous he got. Even to this day, Dan still has difficulty acknowledging his fame. In fact, the young British actor insists that he is just like any normal teenager—well, almost. "I'm kind of just going through what every other teenager goes through—but with posters," he told the *Chicago Sun-Times* in 2004. "It's not as different as people would expect, I don't think, for me, anyway."

When *Philosopher's/Sorcerer's Stone* premiered, there were Harry Potter products on every shelf, including lunchboxes, Lego sets, and specially made jelly beans with the name "Bertie Bott's Every Flavor Beans," mimicking the film's miraculous candy that comes in every flavor from chocolate to ear wax to liver. AOL Time Warner, the company that owned

Warner Bros. at the time, teamed up with a number of other big companies to help promote *Harry Potter* the movie and Harry Potter the brand. Coca-Cola partnered with the film in a $150 million advertising deal that allowed it to sell soda using images from the movie. That's more than the film's entire budget!

The business honchos didn't want a single living being to miss the fact that the Harry Potter movie was hitting theaters. Leading up to the premiere, English newspapers had daily Harry Potter features and tidbits on their front pages. Television news crews crowded around King's Cross train station to film the spot where the Hogwarts Express departs once a year. A survey from that time showed that Harry Potter had jumped ahead of Sherlock Holmes, Oliver Twist, Winnie the Pooh, and even James Bond as the most famous character in British literature. All this didn't go unnoticed by the British Tourist Authority, which published maps of the various historic locations captured in the film, hoping to entice people from all over the world to visit England.

Like the publishers who made sure there were millions of copies ready when a new Harry Potter book hit bookstores, so Warner Bros. made sure the film played in as many theaters as possible when it opened. *Harry Potter and the Philosopher's/Sorcerer's Stone* was set to play in 131 countries, in forty different languages. In the United States alone, *Harry Potter and the Sorcerer's Stone* played on a record-breaking 8,200 movie screens across the country on opening day. Dan was in store for a ride bumpier than any game of Quidditch could ever be.

VIII The Big Time

More than ten thousand fans gathered to scream and swoon when Dan arrived at the world premiere of *Harry Potter* in London. At the momentous event, Dan watched the film for the third time. Although he loved the final product, he hated seeing himself on the screen, especially that evening. "I hate watching myself. I really really hate it," he told CNN, but at the London premiere it was even worse, or as he said, "quite frightening because there were so many people there."

There were a lot of people who would weigh in on this film, but perhaps there was no one more important than J. K. Rowling. She made her firm pronouncement after seeing the film. "I think Dan nailed it," she said in a written statement later published by the *Toronto Star*, "and I am really pleased." Crowds around the world roared.

But not everyone agreed that the film was a hit. The critical reviews were definitely mixed. In Britain, Dan and his fellow cast members received a lot of praise. Still, not every paper liked it. London's *Guardian* newspaper lamented, "*Harry Potter* has joined the pantheon of films judged to be Not as Good as the Book." Back in America, *Sorcerer's Stone* got the big thumbs-down from reviewers. They saw it as just another soulless Hollywood blockbuster. Well, there's no accounting for taste!

Film reviewers weren't the only ones who criticized *Philosopher's/Sorcerer's Stone*. Some adults felt that all the magic and weird mystical stuff in the film seduced young audiences to become fixated on the occult. The British Association of Teachers and Lecturers—a 150,000-member organization—put out a warning that the film could cause children to become obsessed with the dark arts. This controversy had started with the Harry Potter books, which hit the American Library Association's list of the Most Frequently Challenged Books of 1990–2000 for this very same reason.

Dan dismissed those accusations as being completely absurd. "I can't see how it's Satanism or anything," he told the *Toronto Sun*. "The only thing that saves Harry from being killed is the love his mother had for him. How can that be judged as evil?" He explained that the film's central theme was "redeeming love," not "sorcery."

Any controversy over witchcraft didn't seem to keep people from going out to see *Harry Potter and the Philosopher's/Sorcerer's Stone*, that's for sure. It was an undeniable commercial triumph. Blowing the experts' predictions out of the water, the film took in close to $1 billion. Before the film even opened in North America, it had sold several hundred thousand advance tickets, according to reports. There were Harry Potter fanatics who went out and saw the first film twenty-three times! Dan also received a bunch of prestigious awards, including the Variety Club of Great Britain's Best Newcomer Award and Italy's David di Donatello Award.

Along with his awards and praise also came some harsh critiques. Check out the response to Dan's hair, when he was only twelve years old! Because J. K. Rowling had depicted the main character's hair as "all over the place," stylists gave Dan a bunch of haircuts so his hair would resemble that description. But no matter how many haircuts he got, his brown locks always fell neatly into place. Sad to say, Dan had a bowl cut. Most normal kids would only get ribbed by their mates for a bad haircut, but Dan had to deal with worldwide press on his nerdy style. "Daniel has a pudding bowl hairdo," wrote London's *Sunday Express* columnist Anna Pukas. "In fact, he looks like a girl." Ouch! The lame hairstyle wasn't even his choice.

Overnight Dan went from ordinary kid to worldwide star, just as everyone had predicted. Throughout his career he has tried to diminish his celebrity. "I don't really consider myself famous," he told Scholastic.com. "People like Anthony Hopkins and Robert De Niro are famous because they're very experienced and amazing actors." But there was no denying his star stature, which he knew he had to take somewhat seriously. "How many boys my age get to be a part of all these films and have their faces on buses and billboards?" he asked. Not many.

Dan's life became a whirlwind of television appearances on major network shows and at star-studded movie premieres. Big bodyguards and groups of publicists were constantly by his side.

He had come a long way from the little boy who sat between his parents at the theater that fateful night. Despite the exterior transformation, Dan didn't feel that inside he and his young costars were any different from when they had started out. "We probably have changed as actors, but I'm not conscious of myself changing," he related to the *Chicago Sun-Times*. He was proud of this fact and gave a lot of the credit to his parents, who he said didn't lecture, but were there to support him at every step of his remarkable adventure. "My mum and dad have just told me to enjoy it," he told BBC Online. "There are a lot worse things [that could] happen than just being recognized."

Emma agreed with her leading man, telling Blackfilm.com, "I do everything that I used to do. I play sports. I go to normal teenage parties. All of my money is locked away in a bank until I'm twenty-five and I'm not going to see it until then. And I suppose I just have good friends and family who keep my feet on the ground." Out of the three, she felt the most uncomfortable with her massive celebrity. "I don't like the idea of everyone knowing my face or walking down the street and having people say, 'Oh my god, you're Hermione!'" she told the *Ottawa Citizen*. I guess she should have thought of that before starring in the biggest film sensation of the decade!

Rupert, for one, loved all the attention he was getting. "Getting recognized is pretty cool," he said. "I got recognized when I was in Switzerland, up a mountain. That was amazing." There was nowhere these stars could hide, not even on mountaintops!

In addition to getting recognized, these kids got loads of fan mail. Letters poured in for Dan from all over the world. The cast was overwhelmed by the response they received. When any of them had a birthday, those same fans sent lots of presents. "The effort put in is just so amazing," Dan said to the *Toronto Sun* about the thoughtfulness of these strangers sending gifts. However, Dan's mother, Marcia, isn't as impressed by the effort. Every day around 4:00 p.m., she says, the doorbell of their home rings and then she hears, "Does Daniel live here?" She replies yes, but, as she said, "In a tone that will make them never, ever, come back." The fans protest, saying they are carrying presents. But Marcia doesn't soften and just tells them to leave the gifts in the mailbox. "The fans know our address, the names of the dogs, the color of our walls," Marcia told the U.K.'s *Sunday Times*. "I find the level of obsession bizarre."

Because Dan was no longer completely ordinary (come on, riding around in limos with thousands of girls waiting for you wherever you go isn't exactly a typical teen's life), he decided to reinterpret what it means to be a normal kid. "Some people think that because of the [responsibility] . . . that I won't have a normal childhood," he told CBS. "For me, a normal childhood isn't necessarily going to school every day. A normal childhood is just, like, having loads of fun." A lot of kids would probably love to be "normal" according to Dan's definition.

With a tour of premieres all over the world, Dan got to travel to places that few people ever do. Once he even took a helicopter to a premiere! "I feel very privileged to have visited so many countries and seen some of the most amazing sights in the world," he said on the Warner Bros. official Harry Potter website. There was one small downside to all this success: autographs. "I don't like writing my name," Dan admitted to the *Detroit News*. "It's just too long. I have to find a way to write it shorter."

A lot of girls would settle for a kiss instead of

Looking all handsome in his suit and tie, Daniel arrives at the Orange British Academy Film Awards at the Royal Opera House in London's Covent Garden district on February 10, 2008.

Daniel was looking a bit more like a normal teenager when he appeared on *MTV*'s TRL on September 6, 2007.

Daniel, Emma, and Rupert pose for the camera in front of the Grauman's Chinese Theater in Hollywood, California, on July 8, 2007, where the U.S. premiere of Harry Potter and the Order of the Phoenix was held. Check out Rupert's nod to Harry!

Ralph Fiennes, who plays the infamous dark wizard Lord Voldemort, and Dan share in a laugh at the New York City premiere of Harry Potter and the Goblet of Fire. Maybe Ralph is reenacting the rebirth of his wicked character?

Dan and his costar Katie Leung, who plays Harry's love interest Cho Chang, pause for a couple shot!

© 2007 Stephen Hird/Corbis

Looks like Dan and Emma are goofing off in the awards room at the National Movie Awards in London on September 28, 2007.

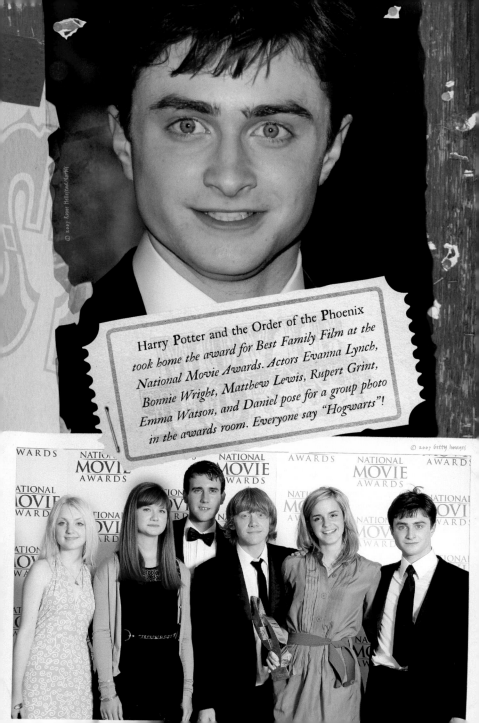

Harry Potter and the Order of the Phoenix took home the award for Best Family Film at the National Movie Awards. Actors Evanna Lynch, Bonnie Wright, Matthew Lewis, Rupert Grint, Emma Watson, and Daniel pose for a group photo in the awards room. Everyone say "Hogwarts"!

Daniel, Emma, and Rupert made their mark on Hollywood Boulevard on July 9, 2007.

Daniel braves the rain at the London premiere of Harry Potter and the Order of the Phoenix on July 3, 2007.

Dan and producer David Heyman pose for a photo op at the Tokyo premiere of Order of the Phoenix.

HELLO
MY NAME IS
Daniel

Dan spotted around London, sporting an army-green cap and a little bit of scruff. Even Dan needs some time out of the spotlight!

© 2002 Haruyoshi Yamaguchi/Cor

STAND CLEAR
ring Operation

an autograph from Dan, if that would be shorter. In the period of time between the filming of *Harry Potter and the Philosopher's/Sorcerer's Stone* and its release, Dan grew two inches and his voice lowered an octave. He was changing from the sweet young kid who had landed the Harry Potter audition and growing into a bona fide hottie whom the girls were gaga over, and these adoring girls would do just about anything to get a glimpse of Dan. But when asked how he felt about being thought of as a hunk, Dan told the *Toronto Sun*, "Personally, I can't actually see it, but if other people can, then great!"

Moving On

Dan didn't have any time to get a big-star attitude from all this attention since filming on the next movie in the series, *Harry Potter and the Chamber of Secrets*, began almost as soon as the production on the first one wrapped. As soon as the first film was screened, Harry Potter devotees were begging for the second one. Director Chris Columbus's kids voiced this impatient attitude. "The minute my kids saw the first film, the pressure was already on me," he told the *Chicago Sun-Times*. "I heard, 'Okay, Dad, now how long do we have to wait for the second one?'"

The second film corresponds to Harry's second year at Hogwarts, where his friendships with Ron Weasley and Hermione Granger pick up at the point they left off. So do the adventures and misadventures that naturally come when a wizard is learning how to master his magic wand. If the first story set up Harry's new life after he escaped Muggleland, then the second one shows that Hogwarts and the magic life isn't always as simple as a game of Quidditch. "The second movie focuses on the fact that his new home and family is in danger and Harry has to save it," producer David Heyman explained to the *Chicago Sun-Times*. "Harry is much more in control this time." Danger lurks everywhere right from the beginning, when Dobby the house-elf warns him not to return to Hogwarts, where eventually he will see many of his fellow students mysteriously petrified.

Chamber of Secrets provided a special challenge for Dan and the team since it is known as one of the least popular books in the series. The first and third books were megahits, but *Chamber of Secrets* had something the others didn't—a superscary scene with thousands of spiders and a gigantic snake. As Chris told the *Chicago Sun-Times*, he jumped on that scene and he developed it into not one, but a few "full-blown, mega-action scenes for Harry and his friends." The action was so intense that Rupert even told the *Toronto Sun*, "I was scared." But

Rupert's main foe was slug slime. "I had to try out all this different flavored slime—orange, lemon, peppermint and chocolate," the always good-natured redhead said. "They made it taste really nice. I quite liked it." That was pretty thoughtful of the production staff to provide Rupert with tasty goop.

Despite Rupert's run-ins with giant spiders and slug slime, Dan really got the best action in this flick. The greatest challenge for Dan, in terms of special effects, was when he had to act opposite an orange ball that stood in for the computerized house-elf Dobby. It's hard to tell what kind of expression an orange ball has. But despite the challenge, Dan enjoyed acting those scenes very much. "I loved doing the Dobby scenes," Dan told the Warner Bros. official Harry Potter website. "I talked to an orange ball at the end of a stick. It was very detailed work because as he bounced around I had to ensure that my eye line was in exactly the right position. It was demanding."

Another difficult scene comes when Harry has to fight a hideous wizard-bred monster, the basilisk, an eighty-foot serpent who lives in the Chamber of Secrets. In real life the crew built twenty-five feet of the monster. "It was hard to fight," Dan told the

Toronto Sun. But this wasn't because the basilisk fought back. "I kept knocking its teeth out. They spent endless hours repairing it."

By the time the second film was in production, the kids had already begun to grow and change, both physically and emotionally. Going through puberty as an actor poses many challenges. Dan's voice broke during the filming of *Chamber*. Luckily, it wasn't so easily detectable in the movie because his voice jumped from one octave to another, instead of yo-yoing up and down like most pubescent boys' voices do. Dan explained that it made his character even more realistic. He laughed it off, telling *People* in 2002, "Harry's also at an age where his voice might start to break, so I don't think it's a big problem."

The first cast had been filled with enough acting greats for ten films, but in the second movie, they added even more. Kenneth Branagh played Gilderoy Lockhart, the egotistical professor of Defense Against the Dark Arts. To fully convey Gilderoy Lockhart's vanity, Kenneth had fifteen costume changes and an office filled with paintings and photos of himself.

Kenneth also proved handy when it came to

preparing Dan for his dueling scene. The young actor picked up his fencing technique from watching Kenneth and Alan Rickman battling it out with swords. "Apparently, there's a certain salute before you start the duel," Dan told Scholastic.com about one of the many cool skills he's acquired since becoming a movie star.

Chamber of Secrets also introduced a new evil character, Draco Malfoy's father, Lucius, who was played by Jason Isaacs. He took his inspiration for Lucius from a real-life conceited art critic. As to his acting method, Jason's motto on this project was the more, the better. "The fetters are off in magic films," he told *Time Out*. "We try to out-ham each other."

Richard Harris reprised his role as Albus Dumbledore, but unfortunately *Chamber of Secrets* would be his last film; he died of Hodgkin's disease on October 25, 2002. Dan was honored to be in the last scene Richard ever shot. "It was awful," Dan told Blackfilm.com of the actor's death. "I don't think Richard is the kind of guy who would've wanted us to mourn over him. He would've wanted us to be happy and just remember him for all the times he made us smile and just laugh." Still, it was hard to go on without him. "He was a perfect Dumbledore," Emma told Blackfilm.com. Michael Gambon, who played the role in the next film, put his own, more mischievous stamp on the character. It must have been hard for Dan to cope with the death of some- one he had worked so closely with, but he perse- vered and continued to use whatever he had learned from Richard's great example.

Everyone worked hard on *Chamber of Secrets*— which hit theaters in the fall of 2002—to make it something they would all be proud of. Like its pre- decessor, *Chamber* also grossed nearly $1 billion! "The second film is even better," Dan told CBS, comparing it to the first. "It's a lot darker and a lot edgier." Dan was also just beginning to show his own edgier side to the world.

Dan Goes Dark

X

If Dan liked *Chamber of Secrets* because of its darker tone, he was ecstatic about the next film on his plate, because it got a whole lot darker. *Harry Potter and the Prisoner of Azkaban*, the third film in the series, which began production on February 21, 2003, has all the usual evil creatures and strange happenings, but this movie goes to even spookier depths as Harry faces the violent death of his parents in the past and a terrifying killer who is after him in the present. To get into this role, where he confronts his demons, Dan listened to the harsh music of the Sex Pistols, a seminal band whose lead singer, Sid Vicious, died of a drug overdose. As if this weren't enough inspiration for an existential crisis, Dan also watched the films of French New Wave director François Truffaut and Italian director Vittorio De Sica, who made *The Bicycle Thief*, in order to understand his character's hopelessness.

To give the film a fresh look that would correspond to the adolescent angst Dan was preparing for, a new director was invited into the Harry Potter family, and the addition was extremely surprising. Mexican filmmaker Alfonso Cuarón—who made a name for himself with an Oscar nomination for his small, subversive film *Y Tu Mamá También*, about two teenage boys who go on a very enlightening road trip—was now put in charge of a mainstream billion-dollar empire. He told *Newsweek* that his version of Harry Potter was going to be a bit more risqué.

Of course, he was only joking. But the new change in director did cause some anxiety among the young actors. Not only was Alfonso best known for making racy films, he also didn't know much about Harry Potter before he got the job. "I hadn't read the books. I hadn't seen the movies," Alfonso admitted to IGN FilmForce. "I knew Harry Potter obviously, but I don't know, for some reason I just thought that it was a big, big kid's franchise. You know? I was not into it." But he changed his tune as soon as he read the script. Alfonso realized just how human these little wizards are. "You can see it as a metaphor about racism and classicism and power," he said. "And also about friendship and loneliness."

Dan, Rupert, and Emma were intimidated by the new director, who blasted mariachi music on the set in England's Hertfordshire countryside to mark hitting the midway point of the shoot. But the original director, Chris Columbus, would never be too far away. He still served as the film's producer. Chris was glad that Alfonso took over. After the first two films, he really needed a break. "My own kids are thirteen, ten, eight, and five," Chris told the *Chicago Sun-Times*. "Ironically, the same people who got me into these films, which are my own kids, want me out. They would like to see their father at the dinner table."

Alfonso was lucky to have Chris's example to learn from. One thing that he learned from Chris was to make sure he scheduled enough time to get the special effects just right in *Azkaban*. Chris confessed to *Newsweek* that the effects in *Philosopher's/Sorcerer's Stone* "weren't up to snuff." Alfonso didn't have to hear that twice. His team worked on just the dementors effects alone for six months.

Of the three young stars, Dan was the most disappointed about Chris's departure. It wasn't that he didn't like Alfonso; Dan had just become attached to Chris due to working with him so closely. Still, Dan tried to look on the bright side. "Everything we learned with Chris, we were now able to put into practice with a different director," he told the *Pittsburgh Post-Gazette*. "And it is harder and more challenging, which is good because if we're getting older and we're not being challenged, there's really no point in doing it."

Producer David Heyman explained that Alfonso had the perfect qualifications for making the film that shows Harry Potter becoming a teenager. "Alfonso has a keen understanding of the nuances of teenage life," he told *Newsweek*. "*Y Tu Mamá* is about the last moments of adolescence, and *Azkaban* is about the first."

Alfonso ran the movie in a completely different way. "Alfonso is much more gritty than Chris ever was," Emma noted to *Newsweek*. "He's really into the idea that [shooting] should be fluid and natural. People can be eating an apple during a take." Alfonso's directions brought out powerful reactions and emotions in Dan, Rupert, and Emma, most of which they didn't even know they had in them. Dan compared Chris's style to that of Alfonso on the

Warner Bros. official Harry Potter website. "Chris is, without a doubt, the most energetic director I have ever met. He was amazing in keeping us motivated and in encouraging us every step of the way," Dan remarked. "Alfonso on the other hand directs in a more intense way. The scenes in the film are some of the most passionate and emotional I have worked on and Alfonso's style has been very helpful." Of course, because the three actors were all older, they had naturally developed a greater acting range, and they could do longer takes and more complicated shots. This gave Alfonso more material with which to work.

Though he was sad about the loss of his original director, Dan was overjoyed about the new additions to the cast. Gary Oldman, one of Dan's ultimate heroes, came on as the wizard Sirius Black, an escaped prison inmate who appears to have an ax to grind with Harry Potter. "He's just the best actor of his generation," Dan said on *Today.* "It was really weird for me, meeting him, because as long as I've been acting, I've always been a huge fan of all his movies. And so it was really surreal . . . meeting him." Before filming started, Emma asked Dan who Gary Oldman was. Dan's response? "Dan almost bit my head off," Emma remarked at a press conference in New York City.

As if Dan didn't already idolize Gary enough, the older actor scored major points when they first met on set. Gary, who knew about Dan's passion for music, presented him with a bass guitar as a gift. Gary is a great bass player himself. That clinched it. Dan's fondness turned into full-on worship as Gary not only gave him the guitar, but a few bass lessons as well.

One of Emma's acting icons, Emma Thompson, also joined the cast, signing on to play Sybil Trelawney, professor of Divination. Thompson, who had been married to another Harry Potter cast member, Kenneth Branagh, for about five years, is one of only ten actors in the world to have been nominated for both supporting and lead actress Academy Awards in the same year. "I love her," Watson gushed to the *Pittsburgh Post-Gazette*. "She's such a great actress, and she did a really good job with Professor Trelawney." Dan is also a fan of Thompson's, as he told *Parade*. "Emma is wonderful . . . and very, very funny."

What marks *Azkaban* as being so different from the first two Harry Potter films is its emotional content. Dan had to show such a range of emotion, all the moods that teenagers go through—loneliness, self-doubt, confusion—only on top of the regular teenage angst, Harry has to fight an apocalyptic battle against evil. "I just kind of took what I was feeling and basically just exaggerated [it]," Dan told IGN FilmForce. During the dementor scene by the lake, where Sirius Black is dying and Harry has to save him, Dan got so into his role that he almost fainted! "I do this kind of stupid thing where I forget to breathe properly," Dan explained on IGN FilmForce.

In *Azkaban*, however, Hermione finally got some action scenes, namely the scene in which she gives Draco Malfoy a serious pummeling. And Emma relished the chance to show the fierceness of her fists. As *Azkaban* was her favorite book, she wanted her performance to be top-notch. For her, this film was all about Girl Power. "I love every single second of it," Emma exclaimed on IGN FilmForce. "I would have done [the punching scene] for a whole week, but, you know, we got it in a couple of takes." Who knew sweet little Hermione was so violent?

The third movie was a turning point in the life and future of the Harry Potter series, as well as in the three young actors' careers. While the first two films got mixed reviews, and the "good" ones were really mediocre at best, the third Harry Potter flick blew its audiences, and the critics, away, making the Harry Potter story into a true cinematic experience. While many reviews called the first two films mere illustrations of the books, critics felt the third movie was strong enough to stand on its own, without the book by its side. James Sanford of the *Kalamazoo Gazette* called *Azkaban* "the most atmospheric, heartfelt, and elegantly eerie installment so far," and "'mischief managed' marvelously." Owen Gleiberman of *Entertainment Weekly* wrote that it was "the first movie in the series with fear and wonder in its bones, and genuine fun, too," and Roger Ebert of the *Chicago Sun-Times* remarked, "The world of Harry Potter remains delightful, amusing, and sophisticated." The Harry Potter series, like its three main stars, was coming into its own, and gaining true recognition across the globe among movie critics and film buffs, not just Harry Potter fans. Now, that's saying a lot!

XI
Keeping Pace with Potter

Production on the fourth film, *Harry Potter and the Goblet of Fire*, began in the summer of 2004 with yet another director, this time a British one, Mike Newell, who directed *Mona Lisa Smile*. The series should have been called *Harry Potter and the Revolving Directors*, but Alfonso Cuarón didn't have any hard feelings. He told *Entertainment Weekly* that he never planned on doing more than one Harry Potter film. "Frankly," Cuarón told the magazine, "I'm extremely lazy."

Prisoner of Azkaban was a critical and commercial success, but Dan wasn't worried about whether *Goblet of Fire* would measure up. He had no doubt it would. "I really do think they're just kind of . . . getting better and better with each film," he told CBS. "The fourth is going to be even better than the third, just because the story progresses even more and you get more into the characters." Not only do the characters get more involved, but so does the adventure. In *Goblet of Fire*, there are dragons, a fierce tournament against other wizardry schools, and a hedge maze that is a lot more threatening than your average shrubbery. *A lot.* "It's fantastic," Dan said to *Entertainment Weekly*. "I can't wait to get the video game for this one."

Not everyone was as sure as Dan of the success of this newest film. Nobody denied the importance of *Goblet of Fire* to the overall series. "This is the hinge," Steve Kloves, the screenwriter, told *Entertainment Weekly*. "This one closes the door on everything that came before, and sets the stage for a new kind of Potter experience altogether." The question was whether they could take this mammoth book and make it work as a movie. The length of the *Goblet of Fire* book (almost twice that of any of the previous books) presented a unique challenge when it came to condensing the tome into a two-hour experience for the big screen. "It's fiendishly intricate. It resists adaptation," Steve told *Entertainment Weekly*. "Far and away the hardest one yet to crack."

Obviously, the situation at hand meant a lot of story lines from the original book would have to be cut for the movie version. One major plotline that quickly got the ax was Hermione's efforts to free the house-elves who worked at Hogwarts. Emma Watson wasn't thrilled that that part about her character didn't make it into the script. "I was disappointed to hear that," she told *Entertainment Weekly*. "But I guess something had to go." Although Emma took the news like a professional, *Goblet of Fire*'s director, Mike Newell, couldn't count on Harry Potter fans being as gracious. And the house-elves were just the beginning. A lot of other elements of the beloved book would have to go, and fans might not like it. "Of course I'm worried. We're talking about a passionate fan base. I won't know if I've pleased them until I put the movie in front of them," Mike said to *Entertainment Weekly*. "Now that will be a very freaky occasion."

In *Goblet of Fire*, Mike planned on concentrating on the main characters' battle with adolescence and not just with the dark arts. Ironically, the actors and their characters were going through the same kinds of experiences at the same time. As Dan told the *Philippine Daily Inquirer*, "[Harry is] coming to terms with a lot of demons and things. He's forced to face them. He's a lot more vulnerable in this film. Sirius can't do anything because he can't come out of hiding to help Harry. Dumbledore doesn't know what's going on. But the main difference is that Harry is growing up and discovering girls."

And what a difference! *Goblet of Fire* was the first Harry Potter film to earn a PG-13 rating. "It's very, very dark and sort of a classic thriller," Mike told *Time*. But its edginess isn't the only adult element. As Dan said, this is the first film in the series where Harry experiences romantic feelings, when he develops a crush on the character Cho Chang, played by the adorable Katie Leung.

A Scottish actress, Katie is not only beautiful but also really smart. In addition to English, she speaks Cantonese and a little bit of Mandarin! The newest member of the Potter gang is also very determined. Other than talent and looks, that's what earned her the coveted role of Cho. Her father had spotted a casting call announcement for *Goblet of Fire* and suggested she attend the open audition. Katie took her dad up on the idea, waiting in line for four hours before it was her turn to perform. Once she got in front of the casting director, Katie only had five minutes to show her stuff. Her chances seemed to get slimmer as the weeks went by without any word from the producers. Winning the part became a distant fantasy. But finally she did receive a call— Katie had beat out more than four thousand girls to become Harry's sweetie, Cho! She told the press that her Scottish accent gave her a leg up on the other girls. But we know it was her energetic acting and bright smile.

Just as *Goblet of Fire*'s story was more complex than the first three, the special effects and lavish sets were also more complex than the previous films. But Dan couldn't have had more fun with it. The movie's tri-wizard competition required the young actor to perform many strange stunts, one of which took place underwater. For this scene, the special-effects gurus built the largest water tank for filmmaking purposes in Europe. According to Mike Newell, it was so hard for Dan to keep his eyes open underwater that they couldn't shoot more than fifteen seconds of film at any given time. And he got two ear infections from all that swimming around. Did that stop Dan from having a blast? As Dan told *USA Today*, "It did sting a bit in the eyes, but other than that and the ear infections, it was fantastic."

In another stunt Daniel had to battle a dragon and slide down a roof fifty feet high to do it! "It was pretty much a vertical drop of about fifty feet," Dan told *USA Today*. "I was on a wire going so fast that my mind didn't have time to catch up with my body and go, 'Wow, I'm falling.'" However terrifying it may have been, that didn't stop Dan from enjoying it, as he continued to say, "It was fun after the first take. But at the beginning, I was absolutely terrified."

Goblet of Fire presented a lot of physically challenging scenes for Dan, but even harder were the emotionally difficult moments. One of the most harrowing scenes in the movie is when Harry has to come to terms with the death of a fellow contestant, and tell the boy's father that his son has perished. "I had to tap into emotions that I personally never felt," Daniel confessed to *USA Today*, "that most people never have felt. Because they were challenging, it does make [those scenes] fun."

Because Dan and the rest of the young actors in the Harry Potter films were growing up off camera as the series rolled on, it allowed them to bring a depth of maturity to their acting and a screen presence that they didn't have in earlier movies. They had more life experience to draw from while they played out their fictional scenes.

That was all well and good, but there was a little problem when it came to the main actors getting older. Dan, Emma, and Rupert were aging at a faster rate than their fictional counterparts. Each film represents a year at Hogwarts, but even with their superfast filmmaking, it took a couple of years for each movie to be made and released. With every film, Dan and the others were getting a little bit older than they are supposed to be in the books, so the pace couldn't let up. Keeping up with the making of these movies was grueling, even for the most experienced directors, crew, and actors.

And most of all for Dan—the star of each movie. It certainly didn't leave him any time to make other films, like Rupert did. "As I film practically every day on the movie, it is pretty impossible to fit in other films between times," said Dan, who does try to take advantage of other creative outlets when he can. In 2002 he appeared as the surprise guest in a London play called *The Play Wot I Wrote*, which was directed by Kenneth Branagh. "It was great fun," Dan remarked on the Warner Bros. official Harry Potter website. "And the first time I had been onstage!"

There was no question that our beloved little kid stars were getting older. The signs were everywhere. While on the set of the third film, during his break from the scene where Harry challenges the ominous Sirius Black, Dan did a drum solo with his magic wand instead of playing childish pranks. Emma placed a sign on her dressing room door that read BEWARE, BABE INSIDE.

Alfonso Cuarón, director of *Harry Potter and the Prisoner of Azkaban*, got the first taste of hormones flying on the set. "You don't need to encourage it. You allow it to be," he told *Newsweek*. "And believe me, they have a lot of it."

With the stars' newly charged hormones and newfound maturity came an interest in dating. So it was only natural that people would start to wonder if Dan and Emma had a crush on each other. Emma had transformed from a little, vivacious pixie into a totally foxy teen. Her hair was always perfectly tousled, and her rosy cheeks and megawatt smile were never marred by a zit. Dan had traded in his girly haircut for his own scruffy look, which even appeared dashing with the tailored suits he favored for public appearances. They looked awesome together, arm in arm on the red carpet.

Dan and Emma had to deal with people butting into their personal lives all the time, and as the stars grow older and more famous, the public interest in their personal lives will only increase. Dan blushes anytime someone asks him about his love life. He has never been tied to anyone special (it's pretty hard to find time for a date when you are racing to make so many movies), but he is interested in girls. And girls are super interested in him. Dan gets shy, and red-faced, when asked about girls he likes, but it's even worse when he's asked about all the girls who like him. At an event to promote *Prisoner of Azkaban* at New York's Radio City Music Hall, Alfonso introduced everyone in the cast and invited them onto the stage. But it was when Dan walked from stage left to center stage that the crowd of girls went wild, yelling and snapping pictures. "I'm not complaining," Dan admitted on IGN FilmForce.

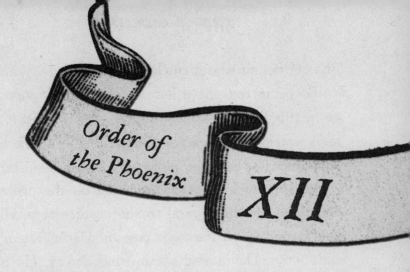

Order of the Phoenix

XII

Dan didn't have much time to enjoy his fans' appreciation of his films (and growing good looks) before it was on to the next Harry Potter movie. Everyone geared up for ten long months of filming as they prepared to tell the fifth story in the seven-book series. *Harry Potter and the Order of the Phoenix*, which started production in the winter of 2006, would be the most expensive film in the series so far. In this tale, the evil Lord Voldemort gains followers and power on his return from exile while Harry and his school chums are forbidden to practice the defensive magic they need to ward off this new threat. Harry, who finds himself revolting against the Ministry of Magic, has never before been so alone and so unprotected. "This one's not comedic," producer David Heyman told *Entertainment Weekly*.

"It's very much about the brink of war."

To bring out the difficult new themes particular to this film, the Harry Potter team looked for a new—you got it—director. *Goblet of Fire*'s director, Mike Newell, brought more of a funny sensibility to the sorcerer's tale, so he passed on the project. After considering several top-notch directors, Heyman zeroed in on the right person: David Yates. In some ways, David was an unusual choice. He had directed mostly television, was hardly known outside England, and had never read a Potter book! "I thought it was a curious fit at first," David admitted to *Entertainment Weekly*. But his realistic style fit well with *Order of the Phoenix*. David decided to take on the mammoth challenge. "[Harry's] been through so much," David told *Entertainment Weekly*. "I was keen to make this a much more psychological, emotional Harry than we've seen before."

David was in charge of the $200 million budget and one of the longest books in the series. Like his predecessor Mike Newell, David faced the obstacles of how to compress an 870-page novel into a 138-minute movie. Again, that meant a lot of cuts to the story, including Ron Weasley's big Quidditch win against the Ravenclaw team and other subplots with Ron, Hermione, and minor characters such as Dobby the house-elf. Die-hard Harry Potter readers wouldn't be happy, but David stuck to his vision. Someone else wasn't exactly pleased with the cuts: Rupert Grint. "I was quite looking forward to the Quidditch stuff," the young actor told *Entertainment Weekly*. "Maybe next year."

Many familiar faces were back on set. Of course Rupert and Emma where there, and so was Jason Isaacs, who plays Lucius Malfoy. Dan's acting hero, Gary Oldman, returned as Sirius Black. There were a few new folks too, including the famous British actress Helena Bonham Carter, who plays the witch Bellatrix Lestrange. Because the book is so long, all the actors worked especially hard to make sure their parts didn't end up on the cutting room floor. "We all want to make the most of all our moments," Jason told *Entertainment Weekly*, admitting that not all the brilliantly acted scenes could stay in the script. "Then you'd have a Harry Potter film that lasts fifteen hours."

All jokes aside, Dan faced portraying the most complicated Harry Potter yet. This version of the wizard left behind any vestiges of little-boy tricks as he stood against black forces. Director David Yates was just the man to get Dan to the level where the young actor could convey these complex emotions of anger and despair. "He pushes me further and more often than I ever have been," Dan told *Newsweek*. "That's nothing detrimental to the previous directors, because I wouldn't have been able to do this before, but David has caught me at just the right moment." Whenever Dan had acted out a tough and important scene in the movie, David would gently approach the actor after he had yelled cut and would privately say, "I think you can do it better, Dan." And of course Dan did do it better. As he put it, "I don't think there's been a moment on set this time where I've walked away after a scene and thought I didn't give it my all."

In *Order of the Phoenix*, Harry makes the final transition from a kid to a teen. And anyone who has a big sister or brother knows that's not an easy time. Anger can often be a huge part of adolescence. All those raging hormones lead to moody teens and slammed doors in real life. Imagine if a teen you knew had dangerous magical powers. Yikes! "He lashes out at his two best friends. But a lot of teens do that because of the intimacy with friends. You know it will be okay," Dan told the *Chicago Sun-*

Times. "Harry can also be selfish now. He feels like he needs to live up to this image of the great defender of all things magical." Harry certainly had good reason to be furious; every imaginable force of evil had threatened his life. Still, seeing tremendous anger bubble up in their favorite wizard freaked out a lot of fans. Dan told the *Chicago Sun-Times* that he had a talk with J. K. Rowling about this issue, and the author assured the actor that Harry "has a right to his anger."

What would any good teen drama be without a kiss? Well, Harry finally gets to act out his feelings with on-screen love interest Cho Chang. In *Order of the Phoenix*, they share a first kiss. While on-screen it might have been all romance and passion, offscreen it was a complete goof fest. In fact, it took them a while to recover from smooching. "I love the scene after the kiss," Dan told the *Chicago Sun-Times*. "We were all in hysterics on the set. It was genuine and all of us were in a giggly mood. We couldn't keep it together."

Dan found a lot to love in *Order of the Phoenix*. For the first time, he was able to look up at the screen and truly appreciate his work. "I actually didn't mind watching myself, for sort of the first time in five films," he told *Entertainment Weekly*. "I have got better. Thank God!" He was never bad, but now Dan had confidence in himself and his acting. With this newfound self-assurance, the young actor was ready for a new challenge. He was ready to explore the world of acting outside of Harry Potter.

Branching Out

XIII

Most actors would kill to be in Dan's place. As the star of one of the most successful franchises in film history, he could do almost anything he wanted. "That's the great thing about Harry Potter, it allows me to not rely on the money thing anymore," he told the *New Zealand Press Association*. "Let's face it, Harry Potter will, for at least the foreseeable future, keep my profile relatively high as it is, so it's nice to be able to branch out." But branch out to what? Would he buy a private island in the Caribbean and retire at the ripe age of twenty-one? No way. Dan hoped to prove that he could do a lot more than just play the part of Harry Potter. He wanted to be a serious actor.

While a lot of actors tend to give phony statements about their work, leave it to Dan to speak the truth. Living high off Harry, he could financially afford to make a few indie flicks. But that didn't mean acting in small, artistic projects would be a breeze. In some ways it would have been easier for Dan to stick to massive movies with loads of special effects. Stripped-down little projects would really showcase whether or not he could actually act. Dan was a victim of his own success. Most of the public associated him with Harry Potter, and separating the real-life kid from his character would be a tricky feat. But the young actor has always enjoyed setting new goals for himself. "Any pressure that I feel," he told the New Zealand Press Association, "has been put on me by myself."

Dan chose the most stripped-down role, literally, to prove himself. For the lead role in a play called *Equus* that was staged in London, Dan had to get completely naked onstage for ten long minutes. That's right. *Completely naked!* "Part of me wants to shake up people's perception of me, just shove me in a blender," Dan told *Newsweek.* Well, taking it all off in front of strangers every night did the trick. "It's a really challenging play, and if I can pull it off . . . I hope people will stop and think, 'Maybe he can do something other than Harry.'" They might also stop and think, "Put some clothes on, Dan!"

That's not all. In his part as Alan, Dan acted very un-Harry-like, for his character had to smoke and swear onstage! One might think that the executives over at Harry Potter's movie studio, Warner Bros., would have been really mad that their young star had chosen such a racy role to prove his acting chops. But they know Dan's a class act and backed him all the way. "We supported him in his desire to stretch as an artist," the studio's production president Jeff Robinov told *Entertainment Weekly*. "There wasn't any real anxiety about it."

Potter producer David Heyman gave Dan's decision to do the play a thumbs-up as well. "I think it shows a young man who is pushing boundaries," he told *Newsweek*. His Potter costars agreed, also supporting his decision to do the play. Emma Watson admitted that when she first heard Dan was going to go through with it, she told him, "You're mad, absolutely mad!" But she wound up calling the decision "brave," bought a ticket to the show, and told the *Sun Herald*, "I was completely blown away."

Emma may have thought Dan was a smash success, but what would the tough British critics, accustomed to the best theater in the world, make of Dan's performance? If Dan was worried before the open-ing night of *Equus* in February 2007, he shouldn't have been. The praise couldn't have been higher. The critics gave him glowing reviews. "Daniel Rad-cliffe brilliantly succeeds in throwing off the mantle of Harry Potter, announcing himself as a thrilling stage actor of unexpected range and depth," raved Charles Spencer for Britain's *Telegraph* newspaper.

The show quickly became the hottest ticket in London's West End (the English equivalent of Broadway). The media frenzy surrounding Dan's part, and how little he wears during some of it, com-bined with the great reviews led to more than $4 million in advance ticket sales. For the next three months, Dan spent eight shows a week baring his soul to eager audiences in a grueling schedule that didn't let up.

Work never scared off Dan. In fact, he wanted to practice the craft of serious acting so much that he squeezed in these smaller projects around the fast-paced Harry Potter production schedule. Instead of taking a much-deserved vacation to the beach or countryside, Dan chose to take on meaningful proj-ects such as a small film, *December Boys*, which he shot in six weeks between *Goblet of Fire* and *Order of the Phoenix*. It must have been weird for him to make an entire movie in less than two months when he was used to the Potter films, which go on for almost a year! "This script was far and away the best I've seen," Dan told the *Dallas Morning News*. *December Boys* revolves around four orphan boys on a beach vacation in Australia during the 1960s.

Since he was trying to stretch as an actor, it's ironic that Dan wound up playing an orphan (this time named Maps) yet again in *December Boys*! "The tally is up to three," he laughed in an interview with MTV.com. "David [Copperfield], Harry [Potter] and now Maps. It's not intentional, it just happens that way. . . . I don't know why I have a knack for them—I had a happy upbringing." But the characters' lack of parents is where the comparison among them ends. His character Maps is nothing like Harry—and doesn't know a single magic trick!

If the other actors on the set of *December Boys* were intimidated by working with the real-life guy behind Harry Potter, they certainly didn't show it. "I got along very well with the kids. They were very relaxed," Dan told the *Dallas Morning News*. Not that the other guys weren't Harry Potter fans. They had seen all the movies and would pepper Dan with questions about how different magical episodes had been brought to the big screen. But after he would share his trade secrets, Dan admitted, "they would be bitterly disappointed. Deep down, I think no one wants to know it isn't really magic."

Even though this was just a small picture, Dan's involvement brought big show business glitz to the whole enterprise. At the red carpet premiere in Melbourne, Australia, in early September, hundreds of hysterical teenagers lined up for seven hours for the chance to see their beloved Harry Potter in person. It was as crazy as any rock concert. Girls screamed out, "I love you!" and one even passed out. A few children had to be pulled out by security guards before they were crushed by the crowd. Everyone involved in *December Boys*, even Dan, was stunned by the turnout. Didn't he know yet that he is one of the biggest stars in the world?

In his next non-Potter project, Dan once again broke out of typecasting. The television drama *My Boy Jack* revolves around the true story of Rudyard Kipling, one of the most popular British authors of the early twentieth century, and his search for his son, Jack, who went missing in battle during World War I. Daniel played the Kiplings' son, Jack.

With *Equus, December Boys,* and *My Boy Jack,* Dan had certainly accomplished his mission—people saw that there was much more to him than Harry Potter. The media began to speculate as to whether Dan would resume his role as the famous wizard for the final movies in the series. While he owed his success as an actor to the role, he had quickly proved that he could do very well for himself without the Warner Bros. machine behind him. The press reported relentlessly about how negotiations between Dan and the studio weren't going well. Perhaps he had outgrown the part.

The fact that Dan's Harry Potter costars hadn't signed deals to star in the final films only fueled the flames. Emma Watson told *Newsweek* she wasn't sure that she wanted to continue acting. In fact, it took some convincing to get her to come back for *Goblet of Fire* and *Order of the Phoenix*. Not everyone is cut out to be a movie star, believe it or not. She was concerned that she couldn't finish the film and keep up with her double major of English literature and philosophy in college. The rumors that Hermione wouldn't grace the screen for the final films spread like wildfire. "It's quite hard to imagine my life without Harry Potter; it's sort of hard to remember my life before. It's sort of taken over," she told the *Sun Herald*. "While obviously it's a huge part of me, it doesn't define me. I know who I am aside from this. But it feels strange that one day it will be over."

Producers, the press, and, most of all, Harry Potter fans, wondered anxiously what would happen if these three favorite actors didn't return.

The End of Harry

XIV

As gossip continued to rage in the tabloids that contract negotiations weren't going well, reports began to crop up that Dan and Rupert no longer got along well with Emma. It looked like the Harry Potter gang was really starting to fall apart. Who knew what was gossip and what was real? With only two books left to be filmed in this long and amazing journey, they couldn't quit now!

Then in March 2007, fans of Harry Potter all over the world blew a collective sigh of relief. The real news was released: everyone's favorite cast was going to be back to finish the series! Warner Bros. issued a statement that Dan, Rupert, and Emma would all return for *Harry Potter and the Half-Blood Prince* and *Harry Potter and the Deathly Hallows*.

Despite all the media speculation about the absurd possibility that producers would have to find a replacement Harry, Dan always knew he would be back to finish up the series. How could he let some other guy take over the role that had made him famous? Sure, there were intense negotiations about the terms of his contract, but that's to be expected in a billion-dollar franchise. "It is important to realize that it's a lot of work and commitment. It can't be rushed into lightly," Dan explained to the *Chicago Sun-Times*. "But the media made more out of if we would sign or not than was true. All of us wanted to come back to finish the series from the start."

That may have been true, but Warner Bros. had to give Dan a huge raise. We're talking *huge*. It was widely reported that Dan received a total of $50 million to act in *Half-Blood Prince* and *Deathly Hallows*. That's quite a bump up from the $320,000 he was paid at eleven years old for his first two Potter films. The British press called him U.K.'s richest teen and estimated that he is worth about $35 million!

Just because he was now a multimillionaire didn't mean Dan would consider slacking off. In fact, he began working on the sixth Harry Potter movie only three days after he finished up the press tour to promote his indie film, *December Boys*. Has Dan ever heard of something called a vacation? Even the young actor had to admit to MTV.com, "That's manic." So Dan embarked on another Potter project that would last ten months, working about nine and a half hours a day in what he called "a marathon, not a sprint."

"We'll get a break at Christmas," he told the *San Diego Union-Tribune* about the *Half-Blood Prince*'s shooting schedule. "And other than that, you're there." Not that he's complaining. He was certainly compensated well enough for his time. But Dan also loves life on set. "It's fun for me because I'm there every day, so you get into a rhythm," he told the *Union-Tribune*. "It's very easy to relax."

Maybe for him. But Emma Watson felt a little differently. Apparently, she wasn't exactly jumping up and down at the prospect of kissing Rupert Grint. That story line was planned for *Deathly Hallows*. "Kissing Rupert's going to be soooo awkward," she told the *Sun Herald*. "I'm trying not to think about it. . . . It's all part of the job, I guess." Lots of girls would kill for the chance to give Rupert a quick peck, but Emma said, "He's not my type." Poor Rupert! What a dis!

Emma was, however, quite satisfied with her part in *Half-Blood Prince*. "Hermione has a massive part to play in Harry's success," she told the *Calgary Sun*. "She teaches him that the only way of defeating Lord Voldemort is through trusting his friends." That's a good message. Rupert didn't get quite as philosophical about the whole project as his cast mates. "There are some really cool bits in it," he told the *Calgary Sun*. "Ron gets a girlfriend in it, so that's going to be quite cool."

There are several newcomers to *Half-Blood Prince*, including nine-year-old Hero Fiennes-Tiffin as the young Tom Riddle and sixteen-year-old Frank Dillane as the teenage Riddle, who will eventually become Lord Voldemort. Jessie Cave stirred quite a controversy when she won the part of Lavender Brown, Ron's girlfriend and fellow student at Hogwarts. That's because producers held an open casting call for girls age fifteen to eighteen, claiming no acting experience was necessary. Casting undiscovered talent has been a tradition with the Harry Potter movies. In *Order of the Phoenix*, a fourteen-year-old unknown Irish actress, Evanna Lynch, beat out fifteen thousand actresses in an open casting call to win the role of Hogwarts student Luna Lovegood. The seven thousand girls who showed up to audition for the part of Lavender had high hopes. But in the end, the part went to Jessie, a professional who was slated to appear in a movie with Oscar-winner Helen Mirren. She didn't even have to go to the open casting call! So you can imagine how mad that made all the people who waited in line for hours to try out.

David Yates was back on board as the director of *Half-Blood Prince*, set for release on November 21, 2008. He predicted the film would be "playful, very witty." Finally, a little rest from all that darkness! "It's much more comedy and the awkwardness of romance," producer David Heyman told the *Calgary Sun*. Emma and Rupert were psyched to hear the news that *Half-Blood Prince* would be a romantic comedy. But Dan wasn't so excited about this happy chapter in the saga. Sure, his costars loved the chance to be funny on-screen, especially Rupert, whom Dan said has "fantastic comic timing." But what about Dan? We know he's one serious actor. "I think the script's great and I think it's going to be a really great film. But I'm just one of those people that, in what I'm doing, I always lean toward the dark side," he told the *Calgary Sun.*

Dan will get his fair share of dark stuff with *Harry Potter and the Deathly Hallows,* which has officially been split into two movies—Part I, set to hit theaters in 2010 when Dan is twenty-one years old, and Part II, set to hit theaters in 2011! Dan seemed to have no qualms about splitting the movie in two. As he told the *Los Angeles Times,* "There have been compartmentalized subplots in the other books that have made them easier to cut—although those cuts were still to the horror of some fans—but the seventh book doesn't really have any subplots. It's one driving, pounding story from the word go."

There's lots of bloodshed as Harry and Lord Voldemort meet up in their final battle, and Dan can't wait for it! "That's the one last hurrah, that film," he told the *Calgary Sun.* "That's going to be great." Dan sure does have an unusual sense of fun.

Just a Regular Kid

XV

You might be surprised to find out that Dan likes to do most of the same things that any ordinary kid likes to do. "As far as I am concerned, I am a normal person," he told the Warner Bros. official Harry Potter website. "I go out with my friends. I go to the cinema—all the normal things that teenagers do. There is an assumption that I cannot leave my house without being hounded. That is not the case. I am able to do many more things than people think I can." When he returns home from the set, it's almost like he was never away, since Dan is really into keeping up with all his buddies through e-mail and text messaging. "All my friends treat me exactly the same as they always have, and we always do exactly the same stuff," he told CBS. In fact, if you were to see Dan at home with his friends, you might very well catch him playing Harry Potter games on PlayStation. "I've been killed by Voldemort a lot," he admitted to *Time Out*.

But, come on, Dan's not *completely* ordinary. When he turned eighteen on July 23, 2007, our superstar received a very special present: a $19 million investment fund that his parents created for him! You could have a really big party with that kind of cash, but Dan kept his celebrating pretty low key. Other than plunking down $17,000 for a custom-made mattress (hey, a big star needs his sleep!), Dan hardly splurged. "People seem to expect me to splash out on a classic-car collection, but I've never been into cars or anything like that," he said in *People*. Time and time again, Dan has said that although he has a ton of it, money is far from the most important thing in his life.

Maybe that's why Dan has stayed out of trouble and out of the tabloids, unlike so many other young stars these days. He gives the credit for his humble attitude to his close friends. "I have some fantastic friends who keep [me] grounded," he told the *San Diego Union-Tribune*. "They keep [me] levelheaded, just because they're honest and they would never pander to me if I was being demanding or difficult or anything like that. I'm not naturally like that as a person at all. Even if I was, they would slap me down." That may be true, but he should also give some of the credit to his parents, with whom he still lives. Dan could live anywhere he wanted—in a big ritzy mansion in the heart of London, filled with flat-screen TVs and other celeb-style furnishings. But he chooses to remain in the simple semi-detached home in the London suburb Fulham that has pro-tected him from getting a big head all these years.

Bunking with his mom and dad also means he doesn't have to worry about cooking or laundry, which is a relief considering his busy schedule. While filming Harry Potter, his day starts at 7:30 a.m. when a studio car comes to pick him up at his home, and he doesn't get home until about 7:30 p.m. It's a long day, so when he gets home from the set, it's straight to the sitting room, where he eats his din-ner in front of the TV (watching *The Simpsons,* of course, what else?). "It's his only chance to unwind," his mother, Marcia, told U.K.'s *Sunday Times.*

Dan's other way to unwind is by watching cricket. While the bat and ball sport, which started in Eng-land and is played on a grassy field, is not popular in the States, it's actually huge in the rest of the world.

"I'm obsessive. Totally," he told the New Zealand Press Association. So much so that when he was in Australia to promote *December Boys*, he came straight home from the movie premiere and went to bed so that he could wake up at 3:00 a.m. to watch a cricket match. That's a real fan. In fact, Dan spent his eighteenth birthday at Lord's Cricket Ground, the headquarters of the world's most important cricket organization. Okay, he's obsessed!

Even though his name and face are known all over the world, Dan still gets starstruck. Big-name celebrities flock to the premieres of his movies, to see *him* on the screen, but Dan still acts like he just caught an accidental glimpse of them at the mall. He said that the best thing about being famous was meeting Ben Stiller, the hilarious comic and star of many funny movies, at the London opening of *Chamber of Secrets*. A close second was meeting the famous couple Tim Robbins and Susan Sarandon at the New York premiere. There are still a lot of people he hopes to meet. They include actor Philip Seymour Hoffman, who has starred in *Boogie Nights*, *Magnolia*, and many other movies. Dan is dying to meet cartoonist Matt Groening. "I'm absolutely obsessed with *The Simpsons*," he told the *Washington Post*.

Sure, Dan's life seems like a dream, but he does have a lot of stresses. Becoming a teenager has only added to them. Still, no one has ever seen him throw a tantrum on the set or slam his trailer door shut. He never fights with any of his costars or crew members. Out of all the millions of fans he's met, there has never been a report of him snapping at any of them. That's because he has a surefire way of dealing with all those new hormones raging within him, as Dan told Blackfilm.com. "Hormones are interesting things. . . . I listen to a lot of rock music, which I think does help to let off a lot of steam, definitely."

Not surprising are Dan's sophisticated tastes. "There's something about Dan that is very much a teenager—discovering music, girls, literature— but at the same time he's very disciplined," Potter producer David Heyman told *Newsweek*. "He reads voraciously and he's an intensely curious young man."

He likes music from bands that broke up way before he was even born. But Dan has been hanging around adults on film sets for a long time now and has picked up a thing or two. He also is the only child of two very sophisticated parents, who took him to the theater regularly and exposed him to a lot. Dan wasn't going to settle for any Britney Spears or the latest boy band. Instead, Dan is into edgier stuff. His tastes are always evolving, but he has a passion for punk music, including the Sex Pistols, New York Dolls, and the Stranglers, all punk bands from when the term "punk" was just invented. "I like the attitude. Yeah!" he told *Time Out*. He also listens to contemporary bands like the Libertines, the Hives, and Franz Ferdinand.

Dan's other extracurricular love is movies—not being in them, although he thinks that's pretty cool as well, but watching them. When he was a little kid, one of his favorite films was *Dead Poets Society*, about young boys coming of age under the tutelage of a character played by Robin Williams. "It's so inspirational," he told the *Rocky Mountain News* in 2001. "That's what first got me interested in acting. The thought of inspiring other people in the way I've been inspired is amazing." Now that he is in the swing of a major acting career, movies provide an escape. In fact, while on break between Harry Potter shoots, Dan likes to lock himself in a small room and just watch films. But don't expect to see him renting a bunch of Bruce Willis action-adventure DVDs. No, just as Dan likes edgy, serious music, his movie tastes also reflect a maturity that is beyond his years. He loves the quirky vision of director Wes Anderson and is crazy for his film *The Royal Tenenbaums*. But his favorite film of all time is *12 Angry Men*—a fifties flick starring Henry Fonda, based on a play about jurors trying to decide whether a boy is guilty of murder.

Since the time when he broke in his reading skills on the Harry Potter books, Dan has expanded his literary interests to an eclectic range. He is a huge fan of Douglas Adams and his cult book *The Hitchhiker's Guide to the Galaxy*, which was recently made into a film.

He also has to keep in shape. Dan has a thin frame that looks great on-screen, but to keep fit, he runs a lot and does push-ups. He plays lots of sports with his friends back home, but their favorite is soccer. Football, as it is known in England, is a national obsession.

When he is on set, far away from his friends and all the diversions they provide, Dan keeps himself entertained. He maintains his movie addiction with a portable DVD player and loads of films that travel with him wherever he goes. And, of course, he practices the bass guitar that Gary Oldman gave him. As Dan told the Warner Bros. website, "It goes everywhere with me." Who knows, maybe one day Dan will form his own rock group. He told Scholastic.com, "I'd love to play in a band."

What's Next

XVI

When the inevitable time arrives for Dan and Harry to go their separate ways, Dan's future will be wide open, and anything is possible. Who knows what he will try next? He's so talented, not to mention handsome, that it's hard to imagine anyone turning him down for any job. One thing is sure: Dan has a long list of things he would like to do after Harry Potter.

Acting is definitely on the list. "I'm incredibly enthusiastic and I love—I love doing it," he told CBS, saying it is definitely a possibility for his future. In the realm of film, he would like to separate himself from the role of Harry Potter, although he knows that reputation will never completely go away. Dan's fine with that. "Harry Potter is such a major achievement that it's not something I want to just forget," he explained.

Though there hasn't been much time in between Harry Potter films for Dan to explore other acting roles, the experiences he has had have ignited in him an even more intense love for acting. In addition to finishing out the Harry Potter film franchise, Dan is involved in a new film called *Journey*, in which he plays twenty-two-year-old Dan Eldon, a journalist who gets killed abroad covering a story. It is also reported that he will reprise his brilliant role in the play *Equus* on Broadway sometime in the fall of 2008.

But acting is only one possibility. From the kid who could hardly make it through a Harry Potter book comes the proclamation that he's considering a life of literature. "I love English, reading, and writing," Dan told *People* in 2002. "I might like to be a writer when I grow up." Or a director. Or a musician—he would love to make a record one day. There's one thing, however, you will probably never see: Prime Minister Daniel Radcliffe. As he told IGN FilmForce, "God help the nation if I'm a politician."

No matter what Dan goes on to do with the rest of his life, Harry Potter will always be a big part of him. He's grateful to be associated with that funny wizard kid, not because the character has earned him millions or garnered him the attention of a thousand screaming babes, but because Harry is a constant reminder that even in real life, anything is possible. "Other than that he's a wizard, he's a really normal person," Dan told the *Philadelphia Inquirer.* "He goes from a zero to a hero, proving that you can do anything."

XVII

Dan's Discography

If you haven't realized it by now, Dan is a huge music fan. "I try my hardest to get as many people into rock music as possible," Dan told BBC's Radio 1. "That's kind of my mission on each film." He's done pretty well at it. He introduced Rupert to the band Kings of Leon. Emma has proved to be a more difficult pupil, however. "Emma's taste in music differs greatly from mine," Dan diplomatically told Radio 1. He did manage to get her into one band he loves, Jet. Of course, his obsession isn't all about the music. He has a ton of crushes on the leading ladies of rock. He admitted to Radio 1 that he is a sucker for Brody Dalle, the lead singer of the punk band the Distillers, who sports enormous tattoos and thick black eyeliner. "I'm madly in love with her!" Dan said. He also professed his love of Marcie

Bolen, the adorable redheaded guitarist for another punk band, the Von Bondies.

Whenever Dan gets a chance in his superbusy schedule, he'll catch a show. He's been to see the Red Hot Chili Peppers with the Pixies in London's Hyde Park, but his first concert ever was the Strokes. The Pixies, the Von Bondies, the Sex Pistols . . . if you have never heard of any of these names before, don't worry. Below is a little history on some of Dan's favorite bands, so that you can get started on becoming a hardcore rock fan just like him.

The Sex Pistols: This band started in the late seventies when guitarist Steve Jones and drummer Paul Cook met vocalist John Lydon—later known as Johnny Rotten—at a shop owned by their manager. The band's in-your-face music often got them in trouble. Their first single, "Anarchy in the U.K.," got the band dropped from their record label. Sid Vicious joined the band as the bassist, although at first he couldn't play his instrument. Even though the Sex Pistols only lasted a couple of years, they changed the history of popular music forever. Their brash sound and raw subjects inspired a massive movement in underground and independent music.

New York Dolls: This group of guys with big hair, which established itself in 1971, is credited with creating punk rock before the industry even came up with that genre. Their loud music seemed to be the parent of two very unruly children named punk rock and heavy metal. Like the Sex Pistols, New York Dolls didn't last long. In fact, guitarists Johnny Thunders and Rick Rivets (later replaced by Syl Sylvain), bassist Arthur Kane, drummer Billy Murcia, and vocalist David Johansen only made two studio albums after coming together, but those records influenced a whole generation of musicians.

The Undertones: This punk-pop band came together in Derry, Northern Ireland, in 1976. Guitarists John and Damian O'Neill, bassist Michael Bradley, drummer Billy Doherty, and lead singer Feargal Sharkey had their breakout hit "Teenage Kicks" in 1978. Their infectious music paid homage to all the ups and downs of adolescence. The band returned in 1983 after a hiatus with *The Sin of Pride*, an album that had a sixties sound to it, but the album didn't rocket to the top of the charts, and the Undertones split up.

The Stranglers: Yet another seventies band, this group started out in 1974 as the Guildford Stranglers in England. Once they shortened their name, they quickly broke out of the small pub circuit they had been playing to perform in much bigger venues. Their music relayed much of the alienation and anger that was typical of this early punk movement. Despite all the controversy surrounding the band's reputation as a bunch of bad boys, their music, including "Peaches" and "Something Better Change," had a hold on the charts. They continued to record music into the early nineties, but their early years remain their most popular.

The Pixies: Although the members of the Pixies weren't accomplished musicians when they began, their band was one of the most influential in the American alternative rock scene of the late eighties. The combination of melodic pop, mysterious lyrics, and heavy guitar licks quickly put them on every indie rocker's listening list. The Pixies formed in Boston in 1986 when roommates Charles Thompson (later Black Francis) and Joey Santiago found bassist/vocalist Kim Deal by taking out an ad in a music trade paper. Kim found them drummer David Lovering. They recorded eighteen songs in just three days in 1987, which eventually got them signed to a record label. They went on to become a worldwide sensation, but rock radio never put their singles into regular rotation. Eventually, tensions among band mates broke up the group in the early nineties.